Craft Candy

Craft Candy

Easy Projects to Stitch, Glue and Paint

Candace Marquette

CINCINNATI, OHIO
mycraftivity.com
connect. create. explore.

Other fine Krause Publications titles are available from your local bookstore, craft supply store, online retailer or visit our website at www.fwpublications.com.

12 11 10 09 08   5 4 3 2 1

Distributed in Canada by Fraser Direct
100 Armstrong Avenue
Georgetown, ON, Canada L7G 5S4
Tel: (905) 877-4411

Distributed in the U.K. and Europe by David & Charles
Brunel House, Newton Abbot, Devon, TQ12 4PU, England
Tel: (+44) 1626 323200, Fax: (+44) 1626 323319
Email: postmaster@davidandcharles.co.uk

Distributed in Australia by Capricorn Link
P.O. Box 704, S. Windsor NSW, 2756 Australia
Tel: (02) 4577-3555

Library of Congress Cataloging-in-Publication Data
Marquette, Candace
  Craft candy : easy projects to stitch, glue, and paint / Candace Marquette.
    p. cm.
  ISBN-13: 978-0-89689-644-4 (pbk. : alk. paper)
  ISBN-10: 0-89689-644-7 (pbk. : alk. paper)
  1. Handicraft. 2. Fancy work. I. Title.
  TT157.M39137 2008
  745.5--dc22
                            2008033474

Edited by Vanessa Lyman
Designed by Julie Barnett
Production coordinated by Matt Wagner
Photography by Don Netzer

METRIC CONVERSION CHART

To convert	to	multiply by
Inches	Centimeters	2.54
Centimeters	Inches	0.4
Feet	Centimeters	30.5
Centimeters	Feet	0.03
Yards	Meters	0.9
Meters	Yards	1.1

ACKNOWLEDGMENTS

Lots and lots of thanks to. . . Krause Publications. To my editors—Candy Wiza, Erica Swanson and Vanessa Lyman—thanks for all of you sticking with me. I know it was hard at times. To Linda Bagby, Alyson Udell and the great team at Duncan Enterprises. Thanks for giving me a chance and helping me catapult my career. You guys have helped make my dreams come true! To Dana Jones at Tandy Leather, thanks for all of the cool stuff. To Olescia at The Container Store, I hope that you like what I did with the canisters. You were so cool to hear me out on my ideas for your product. To Jennifer Green at Saneford Brands, Nancy at Terra Bella Finishes, Shirley Miller at Loew-Cornell, Kyle Sanchez at Robert Kaufman Fabrics, Tracy Whitlock at Fairfield Processing Corp., Peggy Budfuloski at LuminArte, Patti Lee at Sulky of America, Michele DeFay at Wrights Conso, LaRonda Caldwell at Prym Consumer USA, Inc., Terri Geck at Coats & Clark and every other company that had a hand in this book, a great big "Thank You!"

Dedication

To my Lord and Savior Jesus Christ. He makes everything possible. He has been my strength and has taught me so much about myself and how to love others. To my wonderful husband and best friend Shane (aka The Shizznit). I love you so much; you are my heart and soul. Thank you for putting up with me and my creative messes around the house.

To my children Bayley, Bella and Jolie, my beautiful babies, you guys sure do keep mommy busy! To my Dad and Mom, thank you for your love and support. To my beautiful sisters, Chanda and Casey. To Steve and Kathi, I love you guys and I appreciate you so much for taking the children when I was on bed rest working on this book. Doria Sessions, my cousin, thank you for the beautiful hair on these gals. You truly are talented, and you will go far; just remember to keep Christ first and to lean on him for help. You are a wonderful woman and friend to me.

Jaime (aka J girl), thank you so much for your help, creativity and wonderful friendship. What a crazy and cute ball of energy you are! You look so cool in that hoodie; work it girl! Jenny, you look so beautiful, thank you for your help in modeling my accessories! To the girls that modeled for me and helped me put the projects together in the studio: Billie, you look amazing and tough with class. PJ, you rocked the party with that hot pink tube top. What a lifesaver you all were. You all look beautiful and cool in the photos! To Don Netzer, my off-the-hook photographer, you rock Don! We make a great team, and I appreciate all of your hard work and energy. Last, but surely not least, the wonderful makeup artist, April Wilson. Wow, the makeup on the models pops!

Table of Contents

Get Your Creative Juices Flowin'

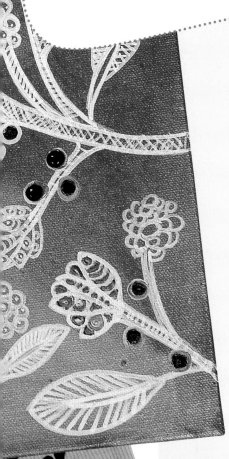

This book contains inventive fashion with a flavorfully sleek mix of elaborate wearable art that has a no-holds-barred attitude. Being creative and finding inspiration in your world can be an unbounded, colorful and zingy burst of excitement. I examine the things around me and get inspiration from life, and I want to challenge you to look around your world. What do you see? What do you smell? What do you feel? Use these things to get your creative juices flowing and get pumped! Figure out what makes *you* tick, and what colors and textures heighten your senses. There is nothing more fabulous than sitting down with all of your crafting supplies and executing a design or idea. In this wild and crazy book, you will learn basic machine sewing, leather stitching, wire wrapping , beading and fabric painting. You will find easy and fun designs through embellishing and mixed media that will spice up your creative world, such as sassy-chic belts, vintagey-glam-rock inspired handbags, accented jeans, artsy pillows, posh-chic wall art, and additional gorgeous accessories and sweet projects.

You will learn how to apply what you have learned to handbags, jeans, cuffs, wall art, hoodies and so much more. I have included templates located in the back so that you will not have a lot of guesswork when it comes to figuring out a design.

I want this book to give you confidence and inspire you to carry what you have learned to future projects. Have fun, and don't feel that you have to follow the directions exactly. These are only suggestions, not rules. Remember, you are the designer and you will be the one wearing and showing off your works of stunning wearable art. So get your hands dirty and let that creative beauty shine.

If you are a beginning designer and choose to only do the beginner projects, no sweat! After you accomplish easier projects with effortless style, you will be confident enough to take on the intermediate and advanced projects. Apply what you have learned and throw your own flavor into the mix because sky is the limit. As you create, I hope that you discover the inner couture gal in you. Get inspired to come up with your own edgy designs and emerge from the boring!

Skill Level Guide

I have devised an easy indicator to let you know what to expect before you start each project. Some of the projects will be suited only for Intermediate and Advanced designers. But don't let that stop you! With this guide, you can identify which projects require which skills, and then you can dabble with new skills to increase your design repertoire. I will show you how to merge all the techniques and combine them with perfect balance. Some will have punchy twists and wild spiky elements. So beware (just kidding)! Have fun, look over everything, and get a zingy eyeful of delectable design adventures!

Have you ever wondered what is the process that the designer goes through to make a design come to fruition? In the next chapters, I hope to give you an opportunity to make something stylish and couture worthy. I want people to stop and ask you where you got it or to assume that you purchased your wares from a high-end boutique. How cool would it be to say to them that you made it? Open up your color palette and color schemes with brilliant energy.

 EASY
This level encompasses simple hand stitching, leather weaving, wire wrapping, beading, painting and blending colors.

INTERMEDIATE
Knowledge of machine sewing, simple embroidery with beadwork, painting and blending will be required.

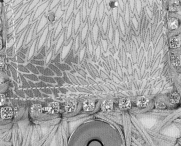

ADVANCED
This will be a combination of all three levels. Don't worry—it will be no sweat for you to get it all down.

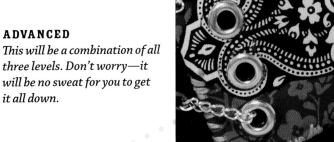

Tools and Materials

There are so many different tools and materials out there to help you achieve your crafty projects. Before you begin, I would like you to look over these pages and get familiar with what you will be working with. This whole experience will help transform your thinking. These versatile tools and materials will help you build a world of knowledge and allow you to open up your creativity. I hope that you will get a taste and a vivid view on how you can achieve your goals in designing. I want you to restyle and maximize your gallery world of art.

I hope that you flourish like a flower and evolve into a more knowledgeable and fearless designer.

READY-MADE CLOTHING ITEMS

Camisoles

Hoodies

Jeans

BASIC CONSTRUCTION NEEDS

Canvas, mounter

Cardstock

Chains—new and vintage in a variety of lengths, styles and weights

Fabric and leather glues

Fabric

Fiberfill

Handbag frame

Leather cord

Leathers

Papers

Picture frame hanging set

Spice canisters

Spray adhesives

Tacky spray

Tape, clear

Tear-away stabilizer—regular and self-adhesive

Tracing paper

Wax paper

Wire—gold and silver

Wooden planks and disks

EMBELLISHMENTS

Beads—pearls, crystal, plastic—both strands and individual

Charms

Clasps and closures

Embossing pads

Embossing powders

Embroidery floss in a variety of colors

Eyelets in a variety of sizes and finishes

Findings, new and vintage—clasps, jump rings, belt buckle blanks

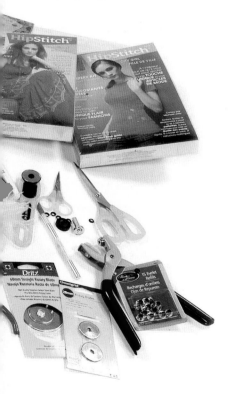

Iron-on transfers

M.O.P. disks and circles

Markers—permanent, art, blendable

Paint mediums

Pants—acrylic craft, fabric

Pendants, new and vintage in a variety of styles and sizes

Pens—metallic, fabric, iron-on transfers

Rhinestones

Sewing threads

Studs

Waxed linen thread

TOOLS

Brayer

Craft hammer

Drill and drill motor

Eyelet setter

Heat-setting tool

Iron and ironing board

Leather hole punch

Needles—fabric, tapestry, machine

Paintbrushes—various sizes and types

Palette

Pliers—needle-nose jewelry pliers, flat-nose pliers, eyelet pliers

Rotary cutter and cutting mat

Rubber stamps of various designs

Ruler

Scissors—paper and cloth

Sewing machine

Stencils

Stick pins

Straightedge

Sturdy work surface

Templates—circles, ovals

Wire-cutters

LEATHER

I don't have a lot of space to describe the many facets of leathers that you can find. I will point out the main things you will need to know to increase your knowledge for these projects when using leather. Leathers are bought by square footage (SqFt), or they can come in:

- **Cowhide Sides.** These soft, cowhide leather sides are a great choice for making bags, clothing and accessories.

- **Premium Leather Trim Packs**. Remnants from handbag makers and more. Excellent for applique, garment trim, wallet insides and hundreds of other projects. They come in assorted colors and small (hand size and smaller) pieces.

- **Garment Cowhide.** Smooth and durable, this leather is great for bag-making.

- **Deer and Cowhide Sides.** These soft leather sides are a great choice for making bags and other clothing and accessories.

CHAPTER

1

Junky Jewelry Box Necklaces

When I go to the antique mall to find vintage jewelry, something intrigues me about the store. My heart starts racing from the excitement, and my mind reels over beautiful pendants and necklaces. For all of these wonderful treasures, I wonder about the person who wore it and what their story is. I often find inspiration from the past and mix that inspiration with the present. I find it so cool how you can take a lovely vintage piece and make it into something totally new. I am giving you an opportunity to open up your jewelry box, or a box of old jewelry, and create something all your own. I want you to remember the person that passed down those pearls, or that beautiful brooch, and make an accessory that exudes the life of the person who gave those precious items to you.

Pretty in Hot Pink Chain Necklace

This necklace is so spunky! I like to think of this necklace as a sophista-punk piece. The hot pink quartz crystals become the main focus of the piece. The pink and turquoise pendant is from a vintage necklace that I took apart. I thought that it might be cool to add it to the chain to soften it a bit. This necklace looks great on a black shirt. The design is so bold and powerful that you really don't need any other accessories.

MATERIALS LIST

5 various silver and gold chains

Wooden plank

1 strand of hot pink quartz crystals

1 turquoise pendant

1 enameled pendant

Wooden pendant

1 sterling silver multi-hole clasp

1 sterling silver clasp with 7 connectors

4 large silver jump rings

Acrylic paint in fuchsia

Butterfly rubber stamp

Drill and drill motor

Needle-nose jewelry pliers

Paintbrush

Ruler

Pencil

*I used a cloisonné enameled pendant.

Drill holes into the top of the pendant, ½" (1cm) apart.

project instructions

1 Attach each end of each chain to the sterling silver clasp holes. When you attach the jump rings, alternate holes so that the chain ends up twisting and creating a layered, knotted look.

2 Paint the wooden pendant with fuchsia acrylic paints, set aside and let dry. (I like to use acrylic paint, because it can create a textured, three-dimensional effect.) Apply black paint to the butterfly, and stamp the butterfly stamp on the pendant.

3 Drill two holes, one on each side of the pendant about ½ inch (1cm) apart. Insert the jump rings into the holes. Keep the jump rings open, and insert each end of the chain to the jump ring. Close with the needle-nose jewelry pliers.

4 Finish off the necklace by adding embellishments such as the turquoise and enameled pendants to the chain.

Tangy Coral Chain Necklace

A good friend of mine gave me the pieces for this necklace. The white beads on orange struck a creative chord in me. I liked them so much that I decided to incorporate them into a new necklace. I wanted to make something funky, offbeat with a modern artsy look. All I did was add several different necklaces and put them together with a handmade wooden pendant. Take what you own, go through your mom's old jewelry boxes, or just find sweet vintage pieces at an antique shop, garage sale or thrift store.

MATERIALS LIST

18-inch (46cm) cable chain, or any chain that you like

Wooden plank rectangle, 2⅜" × 1½" × ³/₁₆" (6cm × 4cm × 5mm)

1 long strand of pearls, or substitute a white plastic beaded necklace

4 small orange beaded strands 14-inches (36cm) long

3 large silver jump rings

1 coral bead

1 bronze coin charm

Acrylic craft paint in green, turquoise and black

Decorative stamp

Drill and drill motor

Metallic gold pen

Needle-nose jewelry pliers

Paintbrush

Pencil

I used a Crafts Etc. Sleeping Woman stamp and Prismacolor Metallic gold pen.

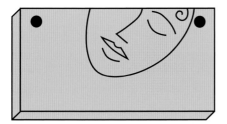

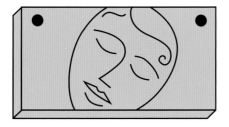

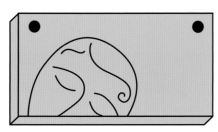

Consider how you'd like to crop the image; try out a variety of arrangements and then pick the one you like best.

project instructions

1 Start with one chain as the base of the necklace.

2 Open one link and attach two jump rings, one to each side of the chain. Add the four strands of orange beads to the jump rings.

3 Take the wooden plank and apply the turquoise paint, then the green paint. Blend together to create a new beautiful color. Set aside and let dry. After the pendant has dried, place the decorative stamp in black paint and press onto the painted wooden plank.

4 Drill two holes, one on each side of the plank at ¼-inch (6mm) from each side. Then insert jump rings into the holes and close with the pliers.

5 Fold the long strands in half and attach a jump ring into the fold of the strand.

6 Attach the wooden plank to the shorter chain by disconnecting one link and attaching the ends to each jump ring.

7 Add the clasp to the chain. Finish off by adding a coral bead and the coin charm to the chain.

Beautiful Chaos

This piece is a combination of necklaces and beaded chain. They are layered to make a whole necklace but are intended to be worn together. When I designed this piece, I wanted to make a statement with the necklaces. This necklace is dear to my heart because a friend gave me some of the charms. One day when I was getting ready for a fashion art show, I realized I needed some sterling silver pieces. My friend told me that she used to make jewelry, and could give me all of her silver crosses. She searched frantically around her house looking for her bag of beads and crosses. When she couldn't find them, she called her husband at work and asked him if he had seen the charms and beads. Surprisingly, he knew exactly where they were. I named this Beautiful Chaos *in homage to her. Sometimes there is no rhyme or reason to her madness, but in the end, her faith and love makes it all beautiful.*

MATERIALS LIST

18-inch (46cm) sterling silver chain

6-inch (15cm) sterling silver wire

2 turquoise beads

1 sterling silver cross

1 turquoise and silver round pendant

Tied jeweled cluster necklace: 2 black and bronze jeweled clusters and 1 old clasp and portion of a vintage necklace

1 starburst pendant

1 silver jump ring

18-inch (46cm) cable chain

21-inch (53cm) sterling silver light chain

7 pieces of sterling silver wire, 2-inches (5cm) long

1 blue and white glass bead

1 yellow freshwater pearl

1 green wooden flat disk bead

1 purple glass bead

1 black vintage disk bead

Chain-nose pliers

Round-nose jewelry pliers

Wire cutters

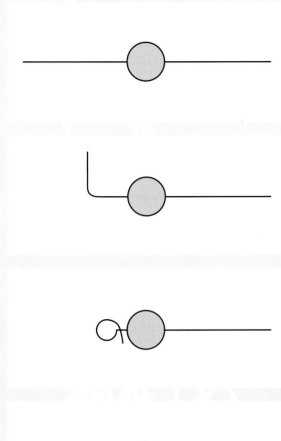

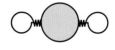

Make the loops with round-nose pliers.

1 With the jewelry wire cutters, cut the sterling silver cable chain in two places. Make sure the cuts are uneven and asymmetrical.

2 Cut the 6-inch wire in half and insert a turquoise bead. Take the round-nose pliers and bend down one end of the wire. Hold one end and wrap the other end around the needle-nose pliers to create a loop. Attach to the chain, and then wrap some wire around the base of the loop. Cut off the excess wire. Repeat step 2 on the other side of the necklace. There are now two turquoise beads opposite each other in the same chain link.

3 Open the jump ring and attach the starburst pendant; now add to the chain. Open the jump ring and add it to the chain.

4 Cut the chain in seven pieces using the wire cutter. Take the chain-nose pliers and bend down one end of the wire. Hold one end and wrap the other end around the round-nose pliers to create a loop. Attach to the chain, and then wrap wire around the base of the loop. Repeat until all of the beads are connected to the chain with wire on the other side of the necklace.

Garden Outcast

Have you ever felt like an outcast? I know I have, and this necklace represents that feeling, but in beautiful and positive way. My friend J-Girl gave me several pieces for this necklace. So we came up with the name Garden Outcast. This necklace is pretty, but it does not quite fit the mold. The colors don't go together, and the materials don't match. But all in all, it creates a pulled-together composition, and I love it. You will not be able to duplicate this necklace exactly, because some of the pieces are rare and hard to find. The steps are so easy and short. So experiment with whatever you find. Gather broken necklaces, chain and pieces of odd jewelry and come up with your interpretation of your garden outcast.

MATERIALS LIST

2 small green beaded necklaces

4 different sized cable chains in vintage gold

2 cerulean blue vintage glass beads

1 white flower pendant

1 vintage gold clasp with multiple attachments

7 silver jump rings

Acrylic paint in Cerulean Blue and Gold

Needle-nose jewelry pliers

Paintbrush

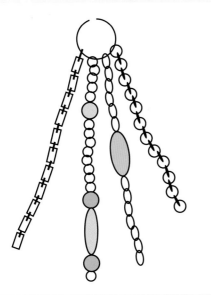

Attach a variety of chains to the open jump ring.

project instructions

1 Attach all of the chain ends to a jump ring. Attach the jump rings to the gold vintage clasp.

2 Paint the flower pendant with a Cerulean Blue wash (watered-down paint). Then with a dry brush, add the gold on top of the blue color. Set aside and let dry.

3 Start by layering necklaces to see how they will hang. Attach the necklaces to jump rings, then add them to the vintage clasp holes.

4 Once all pieces are hanging the way you like, take the flower pendant and insert a jump ring. Add the flower to the end of the very last hanging strand of beads.

CHAPTER

2

Graffiti Graphic Camisoles and Hoodies

OK, no playin', this chapter has a mix of fun, punk-love inspired experimental project techniques to give your clothes that bangin' off tha hezy style that ain't for yo mama!

This is stuff is for the women who love to mix edgy with a bit of girly. So rip through your closets and find a few items that need some spicin' up! Rock on girls, rock on!

Sweet Love Camisole

What an appealing punchy composition with bangin' hues and pretty details. The vibrant patterns of the project scream at you. At the same time, it has a sweetly playful quality to it. In this project, expect rich color bursts and excitement. This one is a graphic print "holla back" chick of a camisole. If you are on a limited budget, no worries! The whole point of this project is to bring joy into your creativity. Trust me, you will find yourself riding on the wings of creative winds.

MATERIALS LIST

White camisole

Fabric paint in a matte finish: azalea, turquoise, green, orange, yellow, black; in a pearl finish: amethyst pearl and deep blue

Tear-away stabilizer

1 flocked iron-on transfer

1 skein of yellow embroidery floss

Size 05 black pen

Size 22 tapestry needle

Scissors

½-inch (13mm) and ⅝-inch (16mm) stencil brushes

2 multisurface stencils, 3" × 5" (8cm × 13cm)

Iron

*I used Tulip Soft Fabric Paint in: Matte, Azalea, Caribbean Turquoise, Granny Smith, Mandarin Orange, Sunshine Yellow, Ebony, Pearl, Amethyst Pearl and Deep Blue Pearl; Tulip Express Yourself! Flocked Iron-on Transfer; Loew-Cornell Synthetic Stencil Brushes; Tulip Multi-Surface Stencil: Heart with Wings, 3" × 5" (8cm × 13cm), and Love, 3" × 5" (8cm × 13cm); Anchor tapestry needle; and Prismacolor Premier Fine Line Markers.

LIKE THE ACCESSORIES?
Project instructions for the cuff can be found on page 52, the necklace on page 14, and the jeans on page 38.

Place the stencils on the camisole to play with the arrangement.

project instructions

1 Place the stencils on the shirt to determine placement. Make sure you leave enough room for the flock design. Place the wings-and-heart stencil on the top part of the camisole. Apply the Azalea fabric paint on top of the stencil with the stencil brush and dab with the paint until the whole surface of the stencil is covered. Wait until dry (about 5–10 minutes) before you lift the stencil.

2 Continue using the wings-and-heart stencil. Use the rest of the fabric paint, mixing them together to come up with your own colors. Try blending the shades together to get a high color impact. Experiment and see what happens.

3 Once you're satisfied with the look, place the Love stencil in the middle of the camisole and apply the black paint with the smaller stencil brush. Use the stars on the Love stencil and apply them in various spots on the camisole.

4 Preheat your iron, and set it aside. Take the flocked pattern and cut it apart. Place pieces in the blank area of the camisole. Arrange pieces in a desired design, plastic side up. Begin ironing pieces to the camisole. Wait until the plastic is cool to the touch before removing.

5 With the black pen, start making circles and random doodles around the painted areas and blank parts of the camisole.

6 Choose several doodles to which you want to add floss. Load the needle with yellow floss, tie a knot at the end, and begin sewing using a satin stitch.

Bling Bling Hoodie Shirt

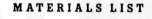

My inspiration came from my daughter Bella's shirt. It had this graphic of a long necklace and some of the beads were embroidered. I thought to myself, "Wow, this is going to be my next project." This hoodie has a young vibe, but is stylish enough for just about any cool chick to wear. It contains a lot of energy with appealing delicate hues and pretty ice cream colors. So open up your junky bags and boxes and pull out those broken necklaces. Mix and match accessories, and use them to create a one-of-a-kind shirt. Go for it, and don't worry if you mess up. Get to it and start creating, girl!

MATERIALS LIST

1 pink hoodie

Tear-away stabilizer

1 old, long necklace

12-inch (30cm) clear rhinestone chain

2 M.O.P. disks

1 round jeweled buckle

1 skein of multicolored purple embroidery floss

Size 22 tapestry needle

*I used a Prym-Dritz Round Jeweled Buckle, Anchor Multicolor Embroidery Floss in Iris, Prym-Dritz Boutique Shell buttons in blue and pink; and Anchor tapestry needles.

Lay out the necklace and rhinestones on the shirt to see where these pieces should hang.

project instructions

1 Place the jeweled buckle near the bottom of the shirt and sew it to the hoodie with the purple floss, passing the needle in and out, and wrapping the floss around the bar.

2 Lay out the necklace and rhinestones on the shirt to see where these pieces will hang. Sew the necklace to the hoodie using the purple floss, making sure that the beginning of the necklace is touching the hoodie's shoulder area.

3 Where the necklace ends don't meet, put the M.O.P. disks and beads in place. This will continue the illusion of hanging jewelry.

4 Sew buttons and M.O.P. disks to the hoodie, and make sure to leave some exposed floss for added character and detail.

sweet note
I used embroidery floss for embellishment, and a cotton shirt, but that doesn't mean you have to limit yourself to that. Experiment, find out what you like, and use whatever strikes your fancy!

Midnight's Dream Camisole

I absolutely adore camisoles. They can be comfy, fabulous or played down. So why not take something so plain and simple and embellish it like crazy. I was drawn to blue hues and felt that this would convey serenity and playfulness. I encourage you to use whatever fabrics you like. But try to keep them in the same color family so the colors melt into each other.

MATERIALS LIST

1 turquoise camisole

5" × 5" (13cm × 13cm) gold-patterned cotton fabric

4" × 4" (10cm × 10cm) blue-patterned cotton fabric

Self-adhesive tear-away stabilizer

30 black plastic rhinestones

3 circular disc beads

2 black iron-on transfers

Cardboard cut to fit inside the camisole

Fabric glue

Spray adhesive

Clear plastic ruler

Pen

White thread

Sewing machine

Iron

I used a Plaid Jean-e-ology Black Flock iron-on and Bird Flock iron-on, Fashion Naturals M.O.P. circles, a C-Thru Ruler; and Sulky Sticky Self-Adhesive Tear Away stabilizer.

Glue the fabric circles to the shirt, letting them overlap a little.

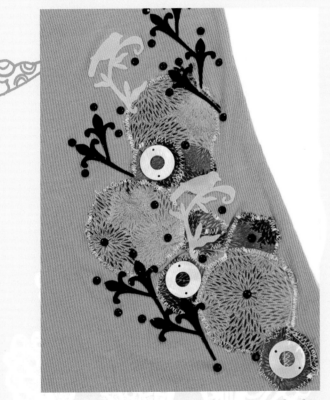

Glue the circular disk beads and rhinestones to the shirt.

project instructions

1 To make the larger circles, use the spray adhesive can or a drinking glass to trace three 2-inch (5cm) circles on the 5" × 5" (13cm × 13cm) piece of fabric. For the smaller circles, trace six 1¾-inch (4cm) on the 4" × 4" (10cm × 10cm) piece of fabric.

2 Cut out the circles. Place the circles on a piece of scrap paper, wrong side up. Spray the adhesive spray lightly in a circular motion. With the camisole lying flat, decide where you would like to place the circles. Make sure they all overlap a little.

3 Set your sewing machine to the zigzag stitch setting. Place the camisole under the presser foot, and sew the circles' edges. Don't worry if you don't stay on the circles. Go crazy with the stitching and make it creative!

4 After you've sewn the circles on, take the black flock design and cut off the branch ends. This should give you four black flock pieces. Cut the blue bird design apart so you have two separate birds perched on a branch.

5 Preheat your iron. As your iron heats up, decide where you would like to place the flock iron-ons. When you decide on the placement, iron the designs to the camisole following the iron-on directions.

6 Randomly glue the rhinestones wherever you want. Lastly, glue the circular disk beads on any fabric circles you wish.

Skater Chic Hoodie Shirt

Hoodies have a California girl flava, so I gave it a bit of funk for character. I love the sense of softness that is twisted with a bit of rock appeal. The colorful designs against the army-green background, and the accents of white and silver studs give it a skater-punk chic vibe. You are going to love wearing this piece. It's kinda sexy but still tough, and I love the way Jaime is flossin' it. Before you start, think about what kind of design you want.

MATERIALS LIST

1 colored hoodie

½ fat quarter yard (23cm × 28cm) in black and white floral fabric

⅓ fat quarter yard (15cm × 18cm) in plum and brown floral fabric

Self-adhesive tear-away stabilizer

Iron-on adhesive

26 silver studs

Art markers in violet, pink, cerulean, yellow and black

White fabric paint

3 skeins of embroidery floss, one each in light blue, yellow and purple

2 multisurface stencils, 5" × 7" (13cm × 18cm)

Stencil brushes

Size 22 tapestry needle

Needle-nose jewelry pliers

Iron

*I used MM-C3095 Black Dandy Damask and EVK-6878-24 Plum from New Traditions by Robert Kaufman; Tulip Soft Fabric Paint in White; Therm O Web HeatnBond Ultrahold adhesive, Prismacolor Art Markers in Violet, Pink, Light Cerulean Blue, Canary Yellow and Jet Black; Tulip Multisurface Stencils: Bird and Love; and Loew-Cornell Stencil brushes.

If you have a black and white fabric, you can fill the white area with color using art markers, as I did here.

project instructions

1 Turn fabric over to the wrong side and iron on the iron-on adhesive to the wrong side of the fabric.

2 Cut out shapes from the fabric, following the pattern or creating your own. The fabric I used here was a black-and-white floral pattern. I followed the design when I cut out the pieces, then filled the white areas with color using art markers.

3 Peel the paper off the back of your shapes, place your designs right-side up on the hoodie, and iron them in place.

sweet note
One thing that makes these Prismacolor Art Markers so cool is that you can blend the colors together. Use blue with pink for a kick of purple.

4 Once the shapes are ironed on, trace around the fabric edges with the black marker.

5 Thread your tapestry needle and sew around some of the fabric pieces, alternating colors.

6 Once you have finished sewing, place a stencil anywhere you like on the front of the hoodie. Load the stencil brush with white fabric paint and dab the stencil until you have covered the design. Peel back the stencil to see if the design transferred. When the design has transferred, repeat with the stencils in any fashion you like and let them dry. Turn the stencil in different directions to give your hoodie a graffiti style.

Use stencils and white fabric paint to create a graffiti effect.

Insert silver studs in the design for a punk accent.

7 Turn the hoodie over and arrange the fabric pieces to make a cool cross, or come up with your own design. Iron them on and trace around the edges of the fabric pieces with the black marker.

8 Insert the studs inside the design, and on the edges and ends to give it a punk accent. Make sure you hold the top of the stud tight when inserting it through the fabric. Use the pliers to close the prongs on the studs. Using the adhesive iron-on, iron a piece of fabric to the inside of the shirt to cover the prongs.

Use iron-on adhesive and fabric to cover the prongs on the inside of the shirt.

Redeem Your Jeans

Look in your closet and select a pair of jeans that you would like to redesign. Pay attention to the colors in your wardrobe to give you inspiration. After you are happy with your choice, start envisioning the look you want to convey. If you don't have fabric, use old clothes to revamp your jeans. If you want to spice up your jeans even more, make jean jewelry to complement them. If you are not comfortable painting on your favorite pair of jeans right off the bat, practice on a piece of fabric. Take a deep breath, relax and just have fun. After you finish, you'll be amazed at what you've created! If you want to be bold and go beyond what the project requires, use multiple templates presented in this book to achieve the look you want.

Rocker Hearts and Butterflies Jeans

This project will completely blow you away because of how your jeans are going to turn out. These jeans have a playful style with bubble gum, popsicle colors. They reflect the right mix of attitude and style that adds to the alluring offbeat feel. I simply adore the girly yet tuff- couture-edgy-punk-rocker-chic style of the design. So rebuke your old style and enter into a world of textile frenzy. Open up your palette with dashes of vibrant patterns and wild, spiky elements and add your personality to the mix.

LIKE THE ACCESSORIES?
Project instructions for the cuff can be found on page 44.

MATERIALS LIST

Rocker Hearts and Butterflies Jeans template (page 122)

1 pair of jeans

6" × 6" (15cm × 15cm) square of geometric black and white print fabric

7" × 7" (18cm × 18cm) square of paisley fabric

Iron-on crystals

Iron-on adhesive

Bead paint in white and gold

7 3" (8cm) pieces of black waxed linen thread

Black permanent marker

Scissors

Needle-nose jewelry pliers

Iron

I used Tulip Bead Fashion Paint in white and gold; AIT-6602-152 Creamsicle Brown Paisley by iota for Robert Kaufman Fabrics; Color Beat AJS-5743-1 by Jennifer Sampou from Robert Kaufman Fabrics; Sharpie Black marker

sweet note
When washing your decorated jeans, turn them inside out. When drying them, place them in a mesh garment drying bag and dry on a low setting.

Iron on the cutout pieces of fabric.

Make sure you embellish the back pockets, too!

project instructions

1 Following the package instructions, iron the iron-on adhesive backing to the wrong side of the fabrics.

2 Cut out a variety of shapes from the black and white fabrics, such as hearts, butterflies and leaves. To create a symmetrical shape—like a heart—fold the fabric in half and cut, just like you did in grade school with construction paper. If you have paisley fabric, you can cut along the design, or cut out clusters of paisley shapes.

3 Set aside some shapes for the back pockets, then remove the paper backing from the rest of the shapes. Arrange the shapes on the pant leg. Think of this part as art. Overlap pieces to punch up the look.

4 When you are satisfied with the arrangement, iron down the shapes. Check the package instructions to be sure, but your iron will probably need to be on the cotton setting (dry setting, no steam).

5 Remove the paper backing from the shapes you set aside, arrange the shapes on the back pocket, and iron them down.

6 Embellish the fabric cutouts with crystals (either gluing or ironing them on following the package instructions). Embellish the front first. If using glue, let it dry, then flip over the pants and embellish the pockets.

7 Using a permanent black marker, trace around the shapes to make them stand out. Feel free to add doodles and designs on the jeans as you work.

8 Using the bead paint, make dots around the doodles on the front side. Let this dry completely (usually overnight), before flipping the jeans over to add bead paint to the pockets.

Gilded Flower Tattoo Jeans

I adore this project because it is so simple yet elegant and artsy all at the same time. How stunning the organic forms of the vines look when they interact with the gorgeous crimson gilded flowers. It creates eye-catching high drama and shines with pops of accented gold. It's so cool to see how the colors play off of each other. The gold eyelets give the jeans a great element of surprise. Spice up anything that you own with this project. You can use this same pattern on a pillow, purse, canvas or whatever you like.

MATERIALS LIST

Strange Botany Flower **template** (page 121)

1 pair of jeans

Gold eyelet kit with 11 eyelets

Long, feathered black tassel

LuminArte Primary Elements Coloring System, 3 teaspoons Hot Cinnamon, 2 teaspoons Mayan Gold, 3 teaspoons Guatemalan Green, 3 tablespoons Simple Solutions Acrylic Medium

Black iron transfer pen

Black permanent marker

Artist palette

White nylon paintbrush

Craft knife

Craft hammer

Iron

Eyelet pliers

Fabric stick pins

Wax paper

*I used a Sulky Iron-On Transfer Pen in black and a Conso tassel.

LIKE THE OUTFIT?
Project instructions for the camisole can be found on page 24.

Use gold eyelets to embellish the flower.

project instructions

1 Photocopy the *Strange Botany Flower* template (on page 121). Trace with the iron-transfer pen. Preheat the iron and use the dry heat setting, not steam. Place the flower template on the left leg of the jeans. Once you have finished tracing the design, cut as close to the design as possible for best placement. Put the template at the bottom of the pant leg and trace. On the right leg, crop off part of the flower at the top and bottom.

2 Place the pair of jeans on a hard, flat surface. Using an iron set on the cotton setting, heat the area where you would like to place the transfer. Once the area is heated, place the artwork facedown on the heated area, pin down the transfer and then hold down in place.

3 Alternate the design anywhere you like on the jeans. At the end of the stem, start drawing swirls around the flower and make dots and circles with the permanent marker.

4 Once the design has been transferred, place a piece of wax paper inside of the jeans where you will be painting so it does not bleed to the other side.
When you are ready to paint, start with the Hot Cinnamon and paint each petal. Let it dry, then accent with the Mayan Gold. Paint the stem and leaves with the Guatemalan Green. Let dry thoroughly.

5 With the black permanent marker, go over the outline of the designs to make the flowers pop.

6 Mark the areas where you would like to see the eyelets with the permanent marker. Poke a small slit at each of these marks. Insert the eyelets and secure with the eyelet pliers. For the final touch, add the feathered tassel.

CHAPTER

4

Bodaciously Tricked-Out Cuffs

In this chapter you will experience making vintage cuffs with colorful fabrics and beads. You will also find gorgeous rhinestone-kissed cuffs that pop with touches of bright color and texture. Make several of these cuffs, and wear them together. After all, strong accessories can completely transform a basic outfit.

You will use basic stitching and embroidery techniques in all of these projects. So practice a bit with a piece of fabric and get comfortable before you attempt making the cuffs. I hope that you find yourself flying on creative wings. Express your tastes in a cool and collaborative way. Take your artalicious and spunky self forward. Make a statement and let your personality shine through.

Hippie Chick Cuff

This cuff was actually a belt that I made in the past. The belt had the right color combinations, but it needed a little something extra. So I added floss to tie off the whole look. Look in your closet and see if there might be something that you could reuse and turn into fashion art. If not, just follow these easy instructions and see what cool cuff you create.

MATERIALS LIST

8½" (22cm) fabric in browns, whites, greens and turquoise

5 miscellaneous pieces of fabric that will fit the longer fabric piece

2 Tulip Glam-It-Up! Iron-On Fashion Designs

1 Tulip Glam-It-Up! Iron-On Crystals in 5mm clear

2 skeins of embroidery floss, one each in brown and light turquoise

Magnetic closure

Fabric glue

Black or white thread

Size 22 tapestry needle

Sewing machine

Scissors

Iron

Flat-nose pliers

Needle-nose jewelry pliers or craft hammer

*I used Tulip Glam-It-Up!- Iron-Ons and Glam-It-Up! Crystals.

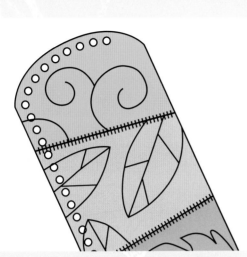

With pliers, punch holes around the edges of the cuff.

Sew floss around the exposed disks until they're covered by floss.

project instructions

1 Glue your miscellaneous pieces of fabric to the longer strip of fabric. Let the glue dry. Make sure the fabric fits the pattern.

2 Place the cuff under the presser foot and begin sewing down the pieces of fabric at each edge.

3 Preheat the iron, and arrange the iron-ons on top of the fabric. Once the iron is hot, iron the decorations on following the directions on the packaging. Lift up the plastic, and if all the pieces have not been ironed on, reapply heat until all of the design has been set. Apply the next one but leave about ¼" (6mm) of space. Finally, iron the crystals in between the iron-ons.

4 With the pliers, punch out 30 to 40 holes around the edges of the cuff. Then punch out holes for the magnetic closures at each end of the cuff.

5 Load the tapestry needle and fill in the holes with the floss. Tie off and sew back under stitching.

6 Insert the magnetic snaps into the holes and then insert the disks into prongs. Secure prongs with the pliers or craft hammer by overlapping prongs on one another.

7 Sew floss around the exposed disks until they're covered by floss.

sweet note
To find the measurements of your wrist, cut out a 5" x 9" (13cm x 23cm) piece of paper. Loosely wrap the paper around your wrist. Where the end of the paper meets, make a mark. Use this as your template.

Tribal Circles Cuff

When I designed this project, I wanted something edgy with a tribal feel to it. This cuff uses big, bold graphic circles, which gives it exactly the right attitude. You will notice the eye-catching texture and stitching. Gold is brilliant against the bright hues. It gives this cuff an upbeat, hippie-punk edge. If you own a charm bracelet or something with chain on it, add it to this cuff. It completes the look without compromising the design.

MATERIALS LIST

Tribal Circles Cuff template (page 120)

5" × 9" (13cm × 23cm) piece of leather to fit your wrist [small: 5" × 6" (13cm × 15cm), medium: 5" × 7" (13cm × 18cm) or large: 5" × 8" (13cm × 20cm)]

Cardboard

29 eyelets

Magnetic snap

2 skeins of tan embroidery floss

Gold metallic pen

Black pen

Art markers in black, blue, mulberry, orange and light olive green

Size 22 needlepoint needle

Scissors

Paintbrush

Clear plastic ruler

Clear plastic circle template

Eyelet pliers

Craft hammer

I used Modge Podge™ and Dritz® Fashion Eyelets, Prismacolor® Art Markers in Jet Black, Copenhagen Blue, Mulberry, Mineral Orange and Light Olive Green; C-Thru Ruler and T-801 Circle templates.

Color the circles with art markers, alternating colors for variety.

Punch out random areas inside the circles and around the edges of the cuff.

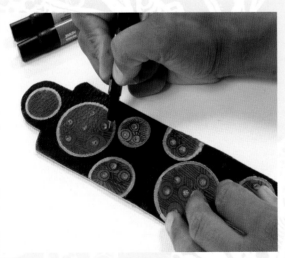

Draw lines and more circles inside the colored circles.

project instructions

1 Photocopy the *Tribal Circles Cuff* template from page 120 and glue it to the cardboard. Lay the cardboard template over the leather and trace around it with a pen, then cut the leather.

2 Using a plastic circle template and a gold metallic pen, create a $1^{13}/_{16}$" (5cm) circle twice, anywhere you like. Then create a $^5/_{16}$" (1cm) circle, but let it be cropped by the leather's edge. Lastly create a 1" (3cm) circle several times to fill up space, cropping some of these circles as well. Color in the circles with the art markers, alternating colors to give variety.

3 Using the eyelet pliers, punch out random areas inside the circles and around the edges of the cuff. With the black pen, draw lines and circles inside the colored circles. Go crazy within the circles. You can make the lines thick or even add your own design. With the plastic circles template, go back over circles with the gold pen.

4 Place fashion eyelets into the holes inside the circles only. Try to evenly disperse the eyelets. Don't overcrowd the circles.

5 At the ends of the cuff, use the prongs of the magnetic snap to make an indention into the leather. First, make a mark with a pen, then pick up the flatter snap piece and press the prongs firmly into the place where you've marked, letting the prong marks be your guide. Use the eyelet plier tool to punch out holes, then insert the flatter magnetic snap prongs. With the prongs exposed, roll the cuff as if you're going to snap it, but instead, press prongs into the leather. This will let you know where the snap needs to be. Place the metal disk into the prongs. On a hard flat surface, hammer one prong flat, then hammer the other prong on top of the flattened one with the craft hammer.

6 Punch holes around the raised snap. Load your needle with the tan floss and thread floss through the first hole and then the next in a clockwise pattern.

Place fashion eyelets inside the circles.

Embellish the edges with tan floss.

7 You will notice the exposed metal disks of the snaps. Choose a hole to start with and begin threading needle though the same holes, except now you will be making a starlike pattern. Keep repeating this step until you cover the disk with floss. Turn the cuff over and repeat on the other exposed disk.

8 Cut a nice long piece of tan floss. Load your tapestry needle with the floss as you would a regular needle. Insert the floss through the hole. Pull the floss downward then back over. Repeat until all the holes along the edge of the cuff are filled with floss.

Sunshine Flowers and Ice Cuff

A bit of ice draws attention when a tinge of light falls on it. It helps to have the right colors to let the light shine and play, such as big, bold floral prints with yellows and oranges that give it exactly the right mix of attitude and style. This upbeat cuff packs a full punch of tangy energy to step up your outfit. When you wear it, it gives you a girly tone that adds a sweet pep to your step. I chose this super-bright floral print for a nice, rich color burst. Watch out, you may lighten up any mood and blow away the people in the room.

MATERIALS LIST

Sunshine Flowers and Ice Cuff template (page 120)

8½" × 3" (22cm × 8cm) piece of tan leather

1 fat quarter yard (46cm × 56cm) of yellow and orange print fabric

Cardboard or cardstock

Tacky spray

Glue

Hot-fix crystals

Magnetic snaps

Strips of rhinestones, two 5" (13cm) lengths and two 3" (8cm) lengths

2 skeins of embroidery floss, one each in orange and sage green

White thread

Fabric paint in yellow and orange

Pen

Craft hammer

Heat-setting tool

Size 16 needle (leather, jean)

Size 22 tapestry needle

Paintbrush

Eyelet pliers

Scissors

Sewing machine

I used Imperial Fushions: Sunshine (EUJ-5905-130); Tulip Soft Paints Matte in Sunshine Yellow and Mandarin Orange; Glam-It-Up! Crystals; Aleene's Crystal Clear Tacky Spray; and Tulip Cordless Heat Setting Tool.

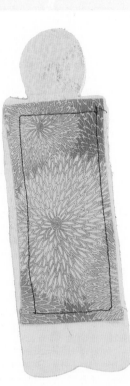

Glue the fabric to the leather, then stitch it down.

project instructions

1 Photocopy the *Sunshine Flowers and Ice Cuff* template from page 120, then glue it to cardboard (to make it sturdier). Cut out and trace the pattern onto the leather, using a pen. Paint the smooth side of the leather with yellow fabric paint. Then mix in a drop or two of orange and let dry. When adding the next color, make sure you blend the colors slightly to give it a slight change in gradient. It's totally okay to come up with different shades. Or, you can just paint it one color.

2 Spray an even coat of adhesive to the wrong side of the fabric, then apply the fabric to the painted side of the leather. Make sure to leave a ¼" (6mm) space between the fabric and the edge of the leather on the flap-end of the cuff. Place the leather cuff under the presser foot. Sew the fabric to the leather, making sure you sew about ¼" (6mm) in from the edges.

sweet note

Before spraying the fabric with adhesive, place it on a magazine and then spray it outside in a well-ventilated area. Just turn the pages for each new piece that you spray.

3 Using the plier tool, punch out holes about ¼" (6mm) from the edge of the leather cuff. Keep the holes about 1" (3cm) apart. Glue a strip of rhinestones along the length of the cuff, and let dry.

4 Load the needle with brightly colored floss and tie the floss at the end. Thread the floss between the rhinestones so it covers the connecting metal strip, but leaves the rhinestones visible. Keep going until you've worked your way all the way around and the floss has overlapped the metal strips.

5 Press the flatter metal snap's prongs in the middle of the rounded part of the cuff until it makes an indention. Use these marks as your guide to punch holes with the plier tool. Once the holes have been punched, insert the flatter magnetic snap prongs. Hammer one prong flat, then hammer the other prong on top of the flattened one. Repeat this step at the other end of the cuff.

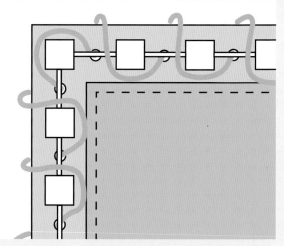

Thread the floss through the holes and over the metal strips connecting the rhinestones.

6 Using the plier tool, punch holes around the raised snap. Thread your needle with the sage green floss and begin threading the floss through the first hole then the next in a clockwise pattern. Cut the floss and move to the next snap. Thread it through the holes. Turn the cuff over and repeat this process for the other snaps.

7 Flip the cuff over again. You will notice the metal disks. Choose a hole and thread the needle through it, only this time, make a starlike pattern over the metal disks. Turn the cuff over and repeat this step on the other exposed disks. Have fun! You can go anywhere with the floss—just make sure to cover the area where the snaps are as much as possible.

8 Follow the directions for the hot-fix crystal applicator. Apply the crystals anywhere you like on the fabric. You are finished, baby! Now you can carry a bit of sunshine wherever you go.

Apply the crystals at random points on the fabric to add a bit of sparkle to your bright, sunshiney cuff.

Vintage Couture Cuff

The inspiration for this project came from the desire to use antique beads and other finds that I had in my possession and integrating them into a vintage-vivid graphic look. I had a lot of fun mixing colors and patterns together. The silver accents give this cuff a polished look. I encourage you to rummage through your old jewelry and use those pieces for this project to make it into your own style!

MATERIALS LIST

Black and white floral print fabric

Yellow and green print fabric

12" (30cm) leather cord

2" (5cm) metal chain link (add a link or two if you have larger wrists)

10–12 assorted beads and findings in turquoise, orange, mustard, green, white, black, gold and silver

2 large wooden beads

10 eyelets, $^5/_{32}$" (4mm)

$1^3/_{16}$" (3cm) ring

Iron

Pen

1 skein of white embroidery floss

White thread

10–14 pieces of black waxed linen thread, each 4" (10cm) long

Craft hammer

Leather punch set, size 6

Size 14 needle

Size 22 tapestry needle

Pliers kit

Fabric scissors

Glass-head pins

Sewing machine

*I used Sofia ZOC 7111-1 White and Imperial Fusions EUJ-5905-5 Yellow fabrics from Robert Kaufman; a $1^3/_{16}$" (3cm) Dritz Glamour Ring; a Tandy Leather Factory Maxi Punch Set, size 6; and a Dritz Gripper Plier Kit for assorted snaps.

sweet note

To find the measurements of your wrist, cut out a 5" × 9" (13cm × 23cm) piece of paper. Loosely wrap the paper around your wrist. Where the end of the paper meets, make a mark. Use this as your template.

Fold fabric wrong side in, then sew the fold closed.

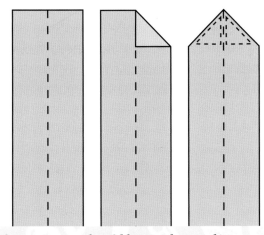

After sewing together, fold corner down and iron. Repeat with other side, then sew as shown.

project instructions

1 Fold the fabric short sides together and pin. Set stitch setting on your sewing machine at straight stitch. Sew about ¼" (6mm) from the fold. Don't worry about getting the lines absolutely straight. Just relax and have fun! Once you've started sewing, remove the pins one by one—do not sew over the pins. Repeat on the remaining piece of fabric. Cut any loose strings.

2 Flip the fabric inside out. Fold over each corner, making a point at the top and iron down. It will look like a triangle. Make sure the edges meet. Sew down the inside corners and bottoms. Insert the pointed end through ring. Fold fabric under, flip over cuff and sew down corners. Fold fabric down at the open ends at ½" (1cm). Fold over again, this time only at ¼" (6mm), then sew down.

3 Place the cuff on a hard, flat surface, such as a wood board or a concrete floor. Flip the cuff over, and at the end where the folds are, begin making marks for the holes. Make five marks about ½" (1cm) apart. Take the leather punch, place on the marked area, and begin hammering. Repeat until all of the holes are done.

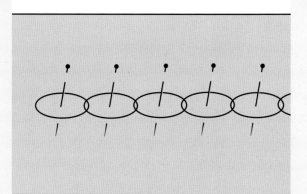

sweet note

Practice on a piece of fabric and be sure to use force when you are hammering. Be careful not to hit your fingers—ouch!

Pin each chain link to the fabric.

4 Place an eyelet in the first hole. Place the pliers on the eyelet and press firmly until you feel a slight crunch. Repeat until all of the holes are filled with eyelets.

5 Grab one chain link and pin it down to the front of the cuff close to the end of the ring. To secure the chain to the fabric, pull the pin through the top of the chain (the pin should overlap the chain) and push the pin through fabric. Repeat for each chain link, and then set the cuff aside.

6 Begin threading the waxed linen through the first bead. Make a knot to hold the bead in place. Then loop through the waxed linen to one end of the chain. Make a loop and tie it off so the bead will be able to move. Repeat this with the rest of the chain links until all the links have beads and findings hanging from them.

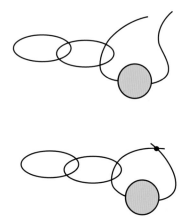

Thread the bead onto waxed linen, then loop the waxed linen through the chain link.

7 Load your tapestry needle with white embroidery-floss. Begin sewing the chain to the cuff, removing the pins as you go. Repeat this until all chain links have been sewn to the cuff. Add detail to the eyelets by sewing around them.

8 Lace the leather cord through the eyelets, beginning with the top left hole. Bring the cord through the left hole. Make sure the ends of the cord meet up evenly. Crisscross the cord and thread it inward then outward. When you are finished, you will see two "X" patterns. Tie a knot about 2" (5cm) from the bottom of the cord. String a bead, and tie a knot under the bead to secure it. Repeat with the other bead and cord.

Accent the cuff with colorful embellishments.

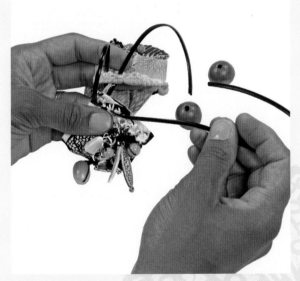

After threading the cord through the cuff, string with beads.

Sweet Moroccan Vibe Cuff

This cuff is one of my favorites. The colors and the patterns used are a modern delight, full of cool collaboration from fabrics and floss. It has a handmade, hippie-chick quality. I merged many looks to create this offbeat motif. This cuff uses vibrant color and texture to give it a youthful look. I hope when you are finished making this beautiful cuff, you will have a great appreciation for what your hands have crafted.

MATERIALS LIST

Moroccan Vibe Cuff template (page 120)

9" × 3½" (23cm × 9cm) piece of leather

16" × 6" (41cm × 15cm) blue, pink and green floral fabric

9" × 3½" (23cm × 9cm)

6½" × 1½" (17cm × 4cm)

Cardboard

Adhesive spray

4 pieces of black and silver beaded trim, two 6½" (17cm) long and two 3½" (9cm) long

2 sets of magnetic purse snaps

5 skeins of embroidery floss, one each in lime green, hot pink, white, orange and teal

Permanent marker

Pen

White fabric paint

Silver ink

White thread

Craft hammer

Size 18 tapestry needle

Paintbrush

Snap fastener tool

Eyelet hand tool

Fabric stick pins

I used Hot Couturier TOC-7114-4 Blue from Robert Kaufman Fabrics; Silver Adirondack Metallic Mixtures; Wrights Black/Silver beaded trim; Black Ranger Ink Embossing Marker, Dritz Eyelet Hand tool; and Dritz Snap Fastener tool.

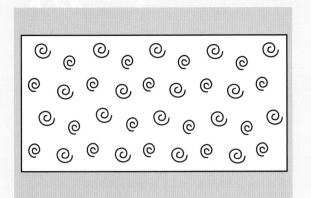

Draw swirls on the painted leather in permanent black marker.

Adhere the fabric to the center of the leather strip.

project instructions

1 Photocopy the *Sweet Moroccan Vibe Cuff* template from page 120, then glue to the cardboard. Cut out the pattern, then use a pen to trace the pattern directly onto the fabric. Cut out the fabric pieces and set them aside. Paint the smooth side of the leather piece with white fabric paint and let dry. Draw swirls with the permanent marker onto the painted leather in a random fashion; set aside.

2 Turn over a small piece of fabric cut out in step 1 and spray with an even coat of adhesive. Apply the fabric to the center of the leather's painted side. Place the leather cuff under the presser foot. Sew the fabric to the leather, making sure to sew about ¼" (6mm) away from the sides of the leather.

3 Flip the cuff over and spray adhesive to the blank side of the remaining piece of fabric. Glue the fabric to the other side of the leather. Place the cuff under the presser foot and sew the sides, leaving about ¼" (6mm). Flip the cuff back over and, using the permanent marker, outline the flowers and stems. Accent using the silver metallic ink. The ink will bleed a little, but that's okay. When adding the ink, try not to squeeze the bottle too hard. You don't want a messy blob on your work. Practice the pressure on a scrap piece of fabric for best results.

4 Take one of the 6½" (11cm) pieces of beaded trim, and place it on the cuff. To hold it in place, use fabric stick pins. Sew the fabric in place. Repeat this step until all the beaded trim has been sewn to the cuff.

Using the permanent marker, outline the flowers and stems on the fabric.

Sew the beaded trim to the edges of the cuff.

Use brightly colored floss to embellish the edge of the bracelet.

5 Starting with the center piece of fabric, with the eyelet hand tool, punch out holes about ¼" (6mm) from the edge of the leather cuff. Thread the lime green floss into the needle, and tie the floss at the end. Thread floss through the first hole. As you go, you will be threading in, under and over to the next hole. Feel free to cover the holes completely with extra floss, threading though the same hole three to four times.

6 Load a needle with hot pink floss, and repeat what you did in step 5 until all of the holes are threaded with the different colored floss. Thread the needle again with the white floss. Thread the floss through the center fabric holes using a backstitch.

sweet note
I embellished the cuff with floss that matched the colors in the center fabric, but contrasting colors could be fun, too.

7 Set the magnetic snap against the edge of the cuff. With the prongs of the snap exposed, roll the cuff as if you were going to snap it, but instead press the prongs into the leather. This will let you know where the snap needs to be.

8 Pick up the flatter snap piece and press the prongs firmly into the place where you've marked. The prong marks will be your guide. Use the pliers to punch out the holes. Insert the flatter magnetic snap into the prongs. Fold the top flap down and then place metal disk into prongs. On a hard, flat surface, hammer one prong flat, then hammer the other prong on top of the flattened one. Measure 2½" (6cm) away for the next magnetic snap, and repeat the hammering process to secure the last magnetic snap.

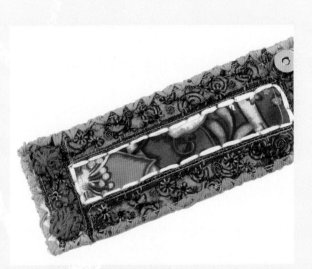

Cover the exposed metal of the snaps with turquoise floss.

9 Flip the cuff over to the decorative side and punch holes around the raised snaps. Thread your needle with the turquoise floss and sew the floss through the first hole and then the next in a clockwise pattern. Cut the floss, then move to the next snap and thread floss through the holes. Turn the cuff over and repeat for the other snaps.

10 Flip the cuff over again. Rethread the needle with turquoise floss, if needed. You'll notice the metal disks. Choose a hole next to the metal disk, and thread the needle though. Aim to make a starlike pattern. Repeat this until you cover both disks with floss. Turn the cuff over and repeat this step on the other exposed disks.

CHAPTER

5

Stunningly Juicy and Edgy Belts

Belts can make an outfit and give it a punch of color and kick-butt attitude—or they can be cute and sassy. In this chapter you will find wild, spiky elements of materials used to create tasteful and chic belts. They give off unbounded bursts of style with wonderful elements of creativity and exuberant color. I adore superbright floral prints with pops of bright color and texture. It is so exciting to create accessories that hang on the verge of sophistication but slap you in the face with a hit of punk, funk and artaliciousness.

Starry Night Snowflake Belt

I like big, bold mixes of patterns, color and media to offset an appealing attitude and style. This belt is straightforward and sweet to the eyes. Accessories like this one are the kinds of statements that can make any outfit look cool and impeccable. It has an unusual tone, but all the while maintains a crisp and unique look with wild spiky elements. I love the color of the bead paint and the effect of it, which actually look like gold beads of candy. I enjoy the pure burst of the flock design. What a complementary delicious treat for the fashion forward!

MATERIALS LIST

2 strips teal spotted fabric, 3½" × 36" (9cm × 91cm)

Tacky spray

White thread

1 ³/₁₆" (3cm) gold ring

1 silver hook-and-eye set

3 flocked iron-on transfers

1 skein of teal embroidery floss

1 tube of gold bead paint

Medium-sized brayer

Iron

Size 22 tapestry needle

Sewing machine

*I used Fusions 11 ETJ-6582-213 Teal by Robert Kaufman; a Prym-Dritz 1 ³/₁₆" (3cm) Gold Glamour Ring; Tulip Express Yourself! Natural Flock Flocked Iron-on Transfers; Tulip Gold Bead paint; Ranger Ink medium-sized Ink Roller brayer; and Aleene's Crystal Clear Tacky Spray.

LIKE THE OTHER ACCESSORIES?
Instructions for creating the cuff can be found on page 52, and the necklace on page 20.

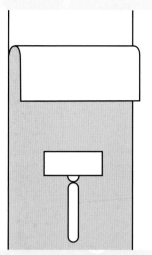

Spray the wrong side of the fabric with adhesive, then, using a brayer, smooth the two pieces together.

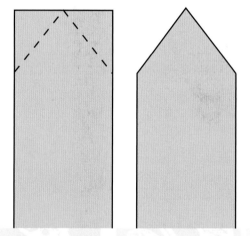

Crease the end of the fabric to create a point, then cut along the creases.

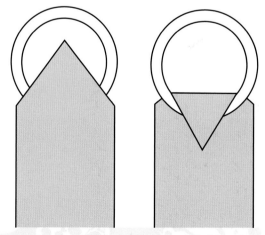

Insert pointed end of the fabric through fashion ring, and then fold down.

project instructions

1 Place the fabric strips wrong side up and spray with an even coat of tacky spray. Pick up one strip, gently lay down the top edge, and match up to the bottom edge of fabric piece. With the brayer, begin rolling down, making sure the fabric is lined up. Once the fabric is secured, roll the brayer over the fabric again, making sure all the bubbles are out.

2 At the end of the belt, fold the fabric into an arrow. Crease the folds using the iron, then unfold and cut at the creases. At the opposite end of the pointed end, insert through the fashion ring. Spray tacky spray and use brayer to smooth down. Make sure that you roll the brayer slowly. Place fabric under the presser foot of your sewing machine. Leave about 2" (5cm) of fabric and sew a straight stitch ¼" (6mm) from the edges.

sweet note
I have the teal spotted fabric sized for a small. For a medium, add 3" (8cm) to the length of the fabric. Add 4" (10cm) for a large.

3 Once you have stitched around the belt, turn the pattern selector dial to H. Set the stitch length dial at 2. Lastly, set the stitch width dial to 3. Start sewing on the very edge of the fabric. The stitching does not have to be straight or perfect; the imperfections are what make some of the best projects. The purpose of this is to complete the edges of the belt. Don't be afraid to experiment with the different stitching widths and patterns.

4 Pre-heat the iron, and set aside. Take the flocked iron-ons, and cut them all in half. Lay down the first piece 2" (5cm) away from the fashion ring, and then iron it down. Arrange the next one and place it at the top about 2" (5cm) from the first iron-on. Repeat until you have an alternating pattern. You will only be ironing five of the flock designs on the front side. Apply the last iron-on 2" (5cm) from the tip of the belt. Once all the iron-ons have cooled, you can remove the backings.

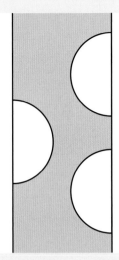

Cut the flock designs in half, then adhere them to the belt in an alternating pattern.

Use bead paint to apply "beads" in a pattern around the flock designs.

Determine where you will set the hook-and-eye closure by wrapping the belt around your waist.

5 Before using the bead paint, test the pressure on a piece of scrap fabric. You want to be determine the amount of paint you'll need to create the right-size bead. Once you have established the pressure you need, apply the bead paint to the belt in a random fashion around the flocked patterns. After you have beaded the belt to your taste, let it dry for twenty-four hours.

6 Put the belt on your upper waist as if you were going to wear it. Pull the end of the belt until the belt comfortably fits to your body. This will determine where you will sew the hook and eye. Once you have established the right fit, make a mark with a silver pen.

7 Thread a tapestry needle with turquoise floss and sew the hook and eye to hold the belt in place.

Bohemian-Inspired Belt

This belt is fun to make. Don't worry about trying to get it exact. If you want to use different fabrics and floss colors, by all means, go for it. Use a graphic element to bring the belt to life. I want to inspire you and encourage you to be your own designer with this project. I used different materials and colors to give the belt its eclectic chic look. I added big, bold graphic pieces and then tied it all together with floss. The chain even adds a sweet twist that gives the belt its spontaneous appeal. When you wear it and add it to a pair of jeans and simple shirt, it will be like wearing a piece of art—so show off your latest creation and watch a crowd start to gather around!

LIKE THE NECKLACE?
Project instructions can be found on page 14.

MATERIALS LIST

3½" × 34" (9cm × 86cm) black floral fabric

3½" × 4½" (9cm × 11cm) line print fabric

1½" × 4" (4cm × 10cm) line-print fabric

3½" × 10" (9cm × 25cm) blue and pink floral fabric

3½" × 11" (9cm × 28cm) plum and brown print fabric

3½" × 6½" (9cm × 17cm) black and white polka dot fabric

7" × 7" (18cm × 18cm) bold graphic floral pattern

4 lengths of silver chain, 2" (5cm) long (chain length will vary for different hip sizes)

4 lengths of brass chain, 1" (3cm) long

Tear-away stabilizer

1 roll of paper-backed adhesive

Gold eyelet kit with 8 gold eyelets

1 brass latch hook

5 skeins of embroidery floss, one each in purple, sage green, pale blue, yellow and golden yellow

Pen

Craft hammer

Craft knife

Eyelet setter

Iron

Needle-nose jewelry pliers

*I used MM-C3095 Black Dandy Damask by Michael Miller; AIT-6604-52 Pistachio from iota; TOC-7114-4 Blue from Hot Couturier; EVK-6878-24 Plum from New Traditions; AJS-5743-1 White from Color Beat by Jennifer Sampou for Robert Kaufman Fabrics; and Therm O Web HeatnBond Ultra Hold.

Iron the graphic cutouts over the fabric, alternating the pattern.

Outline the fabric segments with different colored floss.

Lace the silver chain through the eyelets, then using pliers, secure it to the brass chain. Finish the belt with a hook latch.

project instructions

1 Cut out the patterns and designs from the black-and-white fabrics to be the designs on the belt. Place the 3½" × 34" (9cm × 86cm) piece of fabric face-down and set aside (this will be your base piece). Heat the iron to the silk setting. Roll out a section of the stabilizer. Place smaller pieces of fabric right-side up on to the adhesive side. Move the iron across the fabrics slowly for about two seconds. Cut out fabric pieces from bonding paper.

2 Remove the paper. To loosen the paper for removal, twist the fabric in your hand. Arrange the fabrics as you like, shiny-side down, on top of the long strip of fabric from step 1 (make sure this base piece is still facedown). Iron the fabrics on, moving the iron slowly across the fabric.

3 Once those pieces have been ironed on, take the cutout graphic pieces and place them on any part of the belt in an alternating fashion. Then iron the pieces to sections of the belt. Fold over the ends of the belt at 1" (3cm).

4 Thread your needle with the first color of embroidery floss. Sew the edges of the belt, making the stitches as wide or as tight as you want. Alternate the colors. Finish off the smaller pieces of fabric by outlining the edges with floss.

5 To attach the chain fasteners, you'll need to add eyelets. At the ends of the belt, mark where you will place them. Measure ½" (1cm) from the edge, ½" (1cm) from the sides and ¼" (6mm) from each other. With a craft knife, make small holes in the marked areas. If you prefer not to use the craft knife, use eyelet pliers; the hole won't be big enough, but you can widen it using the end of the scissors.

6 Place the eyelets in the holes and use the eyelet setter to secure them. Starting on one side, loop the chain through the eyelet. Pull through and open the links and secure to the end of the belt. Open both ends of the chain and attach to the ends of the brass chain; repeat on the other end. Add the hook latch.

Candy Cluster Modern Belt

Big, colorful beads and jewels remind me of candy—juicy, scrumptious taste-bud-satisfying gumballs. And black and gold just screams rock star. When making this belt, the sky is the limit! You can use whatever color beads, wire and vintage pieces you want. This is only a suggestion to show you how to get the basics of making this belt.

As for the wire, you can't really gauge how much you will need until you start the project. I suggest buying a whole spool of 24-gauge silver wire in case you mess up or need more wire for beads.

MATERIALS LIST

4½" × 3" (11cm × 8cm) rectangle of black suede

1½" (4cm) square of black suede

1½" × 31" (3cm × 79cm) black mod floral fabric

2 strips of tan leather, 2" × 31" (5cm × 79cm)

6" (15cm) length of leather cord

24-gauge silver or gold wire

Leather and suede glue

2" (5cm) silver rectangle buckle blank

Beads and other vintage findings

8 black fashion eyelets

Art markers in magenta, aquamarine, taupe, orange and mint

Blender marker

Silver pen

White or black thread

Eyelet plier tool

Needle-nose jewelry pliers

Scissors

Sewing machine

*I used MM-C3095 Black Dandy Damask by Michael Miller; a Tandy Leather Rectangle Buckle Blank; Aleene's Leather and Suede Glue; Prismacolor Art Markers in Rhodamine, Aquamarine, Walnut, Orange and Mint Cream; Prym-Dritz Eyelet Pliers; and Snap Pliers.

Place the belt buckle facedown on the black suede, and then trim to fit. (The suede here is a little too big; oops!)

1 To begin the belt buckle covering, spread out a piece of black suede. Remove the belt buckle from the belt, and lay it facedown on the suede.

2 Trace the shape of the belt buckle on to the suede. Add about 1" (3cm) to each side before you cut. Trace out one more piece for the bottom of the buckle. This time, just cut out. You will not need to add more to this piece.

3 Glue the bigger piece to the top of the belt buckle. Then fold over the edges and glue. Glue down the remaining piece on the bottom. You will notice that you can't glue the whole piece down because of the prong. Figure out where the prong is and make a hole with the pliers. Proceed and glue down the rest of the suede. Set aside and let dry.

4 Take the two pieces of tan leather and glue them together using Leather and Suede glue. When these are dry, glue the black suede to the tan strips, and then glue the fabric strip to the suede. Let everything dry. Using your sewing machine, straight stitch the everything along the edge of the belt.

Glue the tan strips together, then glue down the black suede and fabric strip.

5 Round of the ends of the belt using the clear plastic circles template. Trace the top of the circle on the end of the belt, then cut out the half-moon shape. Color the fabric with art markers in whatever colors you like and in any combination. For an artistic feel, use the blender marker so the colors run into each other. I like to match the colors of the beads to the colors that I use.

6 Once the belt buckle is dry, you can wrap it with the wire and beads. First wrap one end of the wire around the prong of the belt to secure it. String the first bead and start to stack, leaving about ½" (1cm) between the last bead and the edge. Wrap the wire around the back side of the buckle, then bring it back to the front. String more beads, embellishments and charms. (I used vintage jewels and chains.) Repeat until the whole buckle has been covered with wire and beads. Secure the end by tucking the end of the wire under another piece of wire.

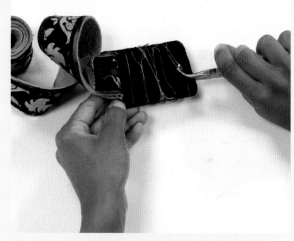

When you have added enough beads, wrap the wire tightly around the back of the buckle and bring it to the front to string with more beads.

sweet note

You can use just enough wire to hold the beads in place, or, if the wire is attractive, you can use a lot as a design element.

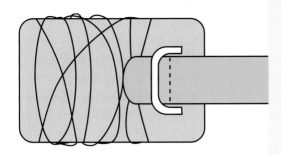

Insert the belt through the bar of the belt, just far enough to ensure it will be secure.

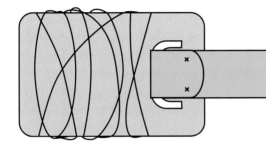

Fold the belt over the bar and mark where you will place eyelets.

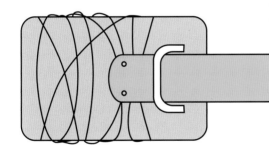

Punch the eyelet holes.

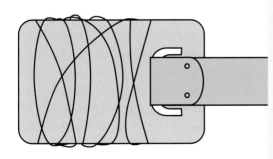

Fold the belt over the bar. Use a pen to mark through the holes to the other side of the leather. Punch through those marks and then finally place the eyelets.

7 Insert one end of the belt through the bar of the belt. Pull the belt through just enough to be able to secure the belt to each other. Measure 1" (3cm) from each edge of the belt. This will give you the exact placement for the eyelets. Make two marks for the eyelets with a pen, and punch out the marks with the pliers. Place a pen inside of the holes to mark the other piece of the belt so that they match up. Insert eyelets into the holes, and then insert the leather cord and tie off.

8 At the other end of the belt, measure 2" (5cm) from the edge and make your first mark for the belt notches. Each hole will be 1" (3cm) apart. Lastly, punch the holes and insert the final eyelets.

CHAPTER

6

Off-Beat Mixed Media Bags

These bags combine colorful fun with sophistication. Some are good enough to eat. In this chapter, you'll find all the delicious, spunky, punk-chic bags your heart could desire. And, yes, you'll look fabulous and sexy carrying one.

Haze of Green Cell Phone Bag

This little cutie is perfect to add that special detail to a purse or pair of jeans. You can also use this mini purse for other things too. The bright metallic green and black give this bag a bold statement. The pops of bright green against the texture of the leather give it an artsy sophisticated look. When attempting this project, be carefree and don't worry if you make any mistakes. Just use whatever you can find in your jewelry box. You can use as many beads as you like to make this project your own.

MATERIALS LIST

Haze of Green Cell Phone Bag template (page 118)

3" × 5" (8cm × 13cm) square black leather

3 black 10" (25cm) leather laces

Cardboard or cardstock

Leather and suede glue

6" (15cm) chain

A selection of beads

Conso green beaded berries

Charms and findings in shades of green

3 or more large jump rings

Large lobster clasp

Silver eyelet kit

Embroidery floss in lime green

1 set of purse snaps

LuminArte Primary Elements Coloring System in Guatemalan Green and Sunshine Yellow

Simple Solutions Acrylic Medium

Sewing machine

Pen

Craft hammer

Needles (size 14)

Sewing machine needle for size 14 jean and leather weights

Paintbrush

Eyelet pliers tool

Needle-nose jewelry pliers

Scissors

Go back twice over what you sewed to ensure that the stitching does not come loose.

Apply the paint to the surface, and then immediately add the Sunshine Yellow to create a blended effect.

Add beads, charms and other finds to the chain to complete the look.

project instructions

1 Photocopy the flap section of the *Haze of Green Cell Phone Bag* template (page 118), and glue it to a piece of cardboard and cut it out. Trace the pattern onto black leather with a silver paint pen and cut out the flap. Mix the LuminArte Primary Elements Coloring System Guatemalan Green with the acrylic medium. Apply the paint to the surface, and immediately add the Sunshine Yellow to create a blended effect. Set aside and let dry.

2 Fold the top and bottom over ½" (1cm), apply leather glue under the fold, and press down for ten seconds. Fold the leather base inside out. Use tape to hold it together. Place under the presser foot and begin sewing a straight stitch ¼" (6mm) from the edge. Repeat on the other side. Turn right-side out and press inside to give the corners their shape.

3 In the upper left corner, ½" (1cm) from the opening and ½" (1cm) from the side, make a hole with the eyelet pliers tool. To open up the hole more, punch again. Insert the first eyelet into the top hole and use the tool to secure.

4 Flip over the base and glue the flap down 1" (3cm) away from the top. Punch holes around the flap, and punch out two holes for the magnetic snap. Install the snap by following the directions on the package. Punch out holes around the snap with the pliers. Insert the leather strip, pull through and tie at the end. Repeat until you have created a starburst pattern. Tie all the loose pieces.

5 Load the needle with floss and tie at the end. Begin lacing up the holes with floss all the way around the closure.

6 Add findings to the chain. Use the remaining leather lace, split it by cutting the lace into two strips, but do not cut it entirely off. Insert one piece through the hole and tie tight. Insert the chain inside the hole, and add beads, charms and findings to the chain to complete the look.

Eclectic Coin Purse

This little handbag has a lot of class with a touch of punk. I like to mix gold and silver together to give my projects that element of surprise! I love the contrast of the supple black leather against the bold black and white fabric. This is your project, so use whatever chain or fabric you want. This little purse will take some time to make, but before you know it, you will have a knockout bag!

MATERIALS LIST

10½" × 13" (27cm × 33cm) piece of tan leather

1 fat quarter yard (46cm × 56cm) green and blue floral fabric

Leather and suede glue

2 lengths fancy silver 3mm cable chain, 10" (25cm) and 8" (20cm) long

13" (33cm) silver 5.5mm curb chain

2 16" (41cm) pieces of black leather cord

Silver or gold square handbag frame

Clear tape

Adhesive fabric spray

4 mm fashion eyelets, 22 silver and 4 gold

LuminArte Primary Elements Coloring System: 4 teaspoons China Black and 3 teaspoons Simple Solutions Acrylic Medium

Pen

White thread

Brayer

Craft hammer

Eyelet pliers

Leather hole punch

Sewing needle

Paintbrush

Artist palette

Needle-nose jewelry pliers

Sewing machine

Straightedge

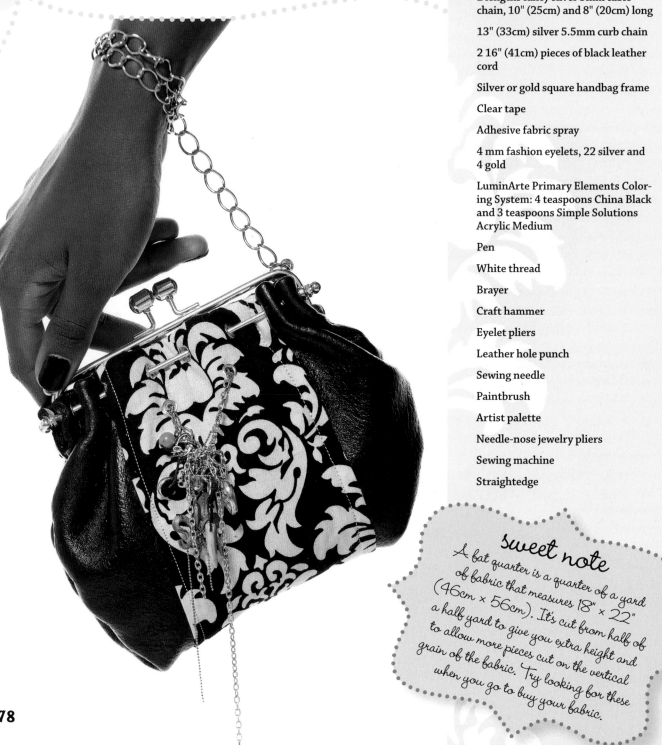

sweet note

A fat quarter is a quarter of a yard of fabric that measures 18" × 22" (46cm × 56cm). It's cut from half of a half yard to give you extra height and to allow more pieces cut on the vertical grain of the fabric. Try looking for these when you go to buy your fabric.

After gluing the fabric to the leather, sew the two together.

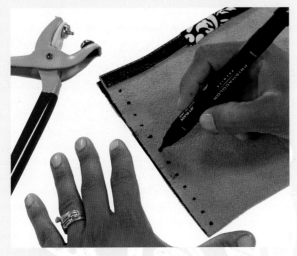

Mark where you will punch holes for eyelets.

Using a leather punch and a hammer, punch the holes.

project instructions

1 On your artist palette, thoroughly mix the Lumin-Arte color and acrylic medium together. Apply the paint mixture to the right side (shiny side) of the leather with a paintbrush. Set aside and let dry. Feel free to use more pigment, but add a little more solution to the pigment as well.

2 Cut a 14" × 5" (36cm × 13cm) rectangle from the damask fabric. Turn the rectangle over to the wrong side and spray with adhesive glue to cover the whole area. Fold the sides, top and bottom down ½" (1cm). Make a nice crease and use the brayer to remove any air bubbles.

3 Apply the fabric strip in the middle of the leather. Use the brayer to smooth out any bubbles.

4 Set your sewing machine to straight stitch. Place the leather under the presser foot, starting on the right edge of the fabric at ¼" (6mm). Begin sewing. Repeat on the left side, top and bottom.

5 Turn the leather over. Starting at the top at ½" (1cm), apply a long line of leather glue on the suede, and fold down. The fold should only be 1" (3cm). Press down with a straightedge for about a minute. Repeat at the bottom.

6 Turn the leather over and fold inside out. Make sure that you do not crease the fold. Be sure that the fold is even and the sides meet. Place a folded piece of computer paper in between the fold to keep the leather from sticking and causing the paint to come off. Tape the fold together on both sides.

7 Starting ¼" (6mm) from the left side, make eleven marks going downward with the pen. Space the marks ½" (1cm) apart. Punch out the holes with the leather punch and hammer. Once the holes are completed, fold the leather in half. Use the holes in the leather as your guide to mark the other side. Punch out the remaining holes.

8 Starting with the top left hole, make ten more marks from left to right, 1" (3cm) apart from each another. Once the holes have been completed, use them as a guide for the holes on the other side. Mark them with your pen and punch them out. For the remaining holes, find the three holes located on the fabric strip. Measure 1" (3cm) downward, starting with the left hole, and mark. Mark under the right hole. Punch out the remaining holes.

9 Place the gold eyelets only in the top and bottom holes. Place the silver eyelets in the last three holes.

10 Starting on the bottom left corner of the leather, thread the leather cord through the hole. Once you get to the end, leave about 2" (5cm) of cord and tie a knot. Pull through until the knot hits the suede. Thread the cord upward, in and out. Pull tightly so that the leather gathers. Stop threading at the sixth hole, and repeat on the other side. Do not cut the leftover cord. Watch the cord and make sure it does not twist. If it twists, it will be difficult to pull the fabric, causing it to bunch.

11 Take one purse frame bar and unscrew the end cap. Insert the bar through the first hole on the left side, then thread it through the holes, bunching the leather together. Once the bar is all the way through, insert the bar into the metal ring of the frame. Replace the end cap, and repeat on the other side.

Securely place eyelets into the holes. Press firmly with the plier tool.

Thread bar through the gold eyelet holes.

Add a gold chain for the shoulder strap and embellish with charms.

12 Wrap the remaining leather cord around the inner purse frame. Pull the leather cord through to the next hole, going upward and repeating until the purse is snug against the frame. Repeat on the other side. Cut the last of the cord and glue it to the inside of the bag.

13 Insert one end of the 10" (25cm) silver cable chain into the first hole, and then bring it back through the other hole. Pull the hanging chain and knot. Insert the 10" (25cm) silver cable chain the same way, and knot. Next, take the 8" (20cm) gold chain, insert through, and knot. Finally, take the curb chain and open up the end with the needle-nose jewelry pliers. Insert the open side through one of the rings where the handle goes and close securely. Repeat on the other side.

To attach embellishments with charms, add them to a hanging chain and attach the chain to the purse using jump rings.

Blue Candy Python Clutch

This clutch reminds me of sugary, tasty candy with an exotic look. It's yummy and eccentric, and you kind of want to sink your teeth into it! I love bright and colorful things, so I wanted materials that I could use for maximum impact. After being inspired by my favorite fashion magazines, I decided to add python and paint into the mix. I know, it sounds kind of wild and scary, but not to worry—you can swap real python for faux python, another funky material or a bold graphic print instead.

MATERIALS LIST

11½" × 11½" (29cm × 29cm) piece of tan leather

9" × 9" (23cm × 23cm) piece of black suede

5½" × 10" (14cm × 25cm) piece of real or imitation python skin

2 strips of black leather, 12" × ½" (30cm × 1cm)

Leather glue

¾" (19mm) silver magnetic snaps

28 black or silver fashion eyelets

LuminArte Primary Elements Coloring System: ⅛ teaspoon (.6ml) Teal Zircon, ⅛ teaspoon (.6ml) Majestic Blue, and 3 teaspoons (15ml) Simple Solutions Acrylic Medium

Pen

Brayer

Craft hammer

Eyelet pliers

Leather hole punch

Paintbrush

Artist palette

Needle-nose jewelry pliers

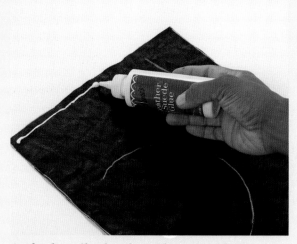

Apply a line of leather glue to the wrong side of the suede.

Fold the edge of the suede over the glue and press firmly.

project instructions

1 Start with the 11½" × 11½" (29cm × 29cm) piece of leather. Place it right-side up, with the shiny side facing you. On your artist palette, mix the LuminArte colors together thoroughly. Apply the paint mixture to the shiny part of the leather with a paintbrush and let dry. Set aside.

sweet note

When mixing the solution and colors, add as much or as little color as you want. The more pigment that you add, the richer the colors will be. The more solution you add, the less color you will have to work with. The colors will become opaque.

2 Place the 9" × 9" (23cm × 23cm) piece of suede wrong-side up. Apply a line of leather glue about ½" (1cm) from the top edge. Fold the edge over ½" (1cm) and press down for about fifteen seconds. Repeat on the bottom. Set aside and let dry.

3 Repeat step 2: Turn over the painted leather piece to the suede side. Apply a line of leather glue about ½" (1cm) from the top edge. Fold the edge over ½" (1cm) and press down firmly for about fifteen seconds. Repeat this step on the bottom, let dry.

sweet note

Don't overdo the glue. If you use too much glue, it will seep out of the fold when you press down, causing it to dry very slowly.

4 Turn your python strip over to the wrong side, and apply glue to only the middle section by making an "X." (Don't place glue all over the python just yet. Only the middle section will need to be glued for this step.) Place the painted leather piece right-side up, and apply the glued side of the python to the center of the painted leather. Press down firmly with the brayer and smooth out to prevent bubbles from forming, and let dry.

5 Turn over to the unpainted side of the painted leather piece, then set aside. Take the black suede, turn over to the wrong side (the shiny side), and apply leather glue to the middle section only by making an "X" or just enough to cover the area. Carefully glue the black suede to the unpainted side of the leather. Smooth with brayer to prevent bubbles from forming, and let dry for ten minutes.

Apply an "X" of glue to the wrong side of the python piece.

Apply the glued side of the python to the center of the painted leather. Press down firmly with brayer to smooth out any bubbles.

sweet note
Python starts very narrow and widens toward the middle. So when you cut your python strip, it could be anywhere from 4" (10cm) to 7" (18cm) wide.

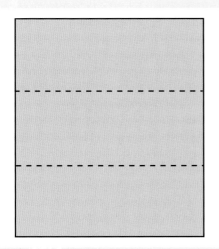

Position the leather lengthwise. Make sure your folds will be appropriately spaced.

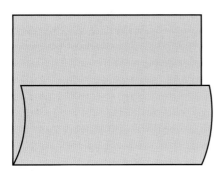

Fold the bottom up first.

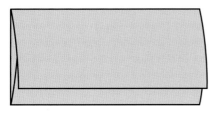

Fold the top down over the bottom. The top should not be longer than the bottom.

6 Now that the pieces of leather are glued, gently fold the clutch into three parts. On the top part of the flap, locate the middle section by folding the pieces in half. As you find the middle of the top flap for the snap, determine how high the snap of the purse should be. Make a small dot in the center. This is where the snap will go.

Practice this step on a piece of paper so that you can decide where you would like to place the snap before committing to it on your project.

sweet note
When folding, do not crease the folds. The bag will look rough, rather than rounded and smooth.

7 Pick up the flatter snap piece, and press the prongs firmly into the marked area. The prong marks will be your guide. Using the plier tool, make two holes into the leather and the suede, but be sure you do not puncture the python.

8 Glue down the top suede part. Insert the flat magnetic snap prongs into holes. Fold the top flap down and place a metal disk into the prongs. Hammer one prong flat, then hammer the other prong on top of the flattened one.

9 Fit the remaining magnetic snap to the newly installed snap. Fold the top flap over, and press the prongs firmly into the clutch. Once you have made a mark, remove the loose magnetic snap piece.

10 Rotate top to bottom, and flip the clutch over. Glue the remaining python to the clutch. Press down with the brayer and smooth out, let dry for about ten minutes. Flip the clutch back over. Glue any excess python to the inside. Be sure not to glue it to the suede. Let dry for ten minutes. Pull back the suede and apply glue, working your way upward and smoothing with the brayer as you go. The suede will cover up some of the python. Let dry for ten minutes.

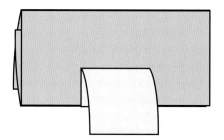

Apply glue to the remaining, unglued areas of the python.

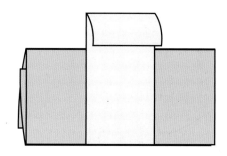

Press the glued python down using a brayer.

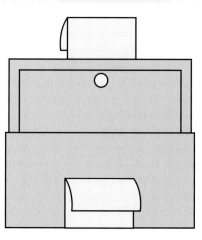

Flip the clutch over. There should be a remaining flap of python on either side that can be folded under the suede.

Once the snap is in place, glue the suede over the python.

You can use jewelry pliers to help pull the leather strips through.

11 Starting at the bottom flap, use your plier tool to punch through the marks, making sure you do not puncture the black suede. Insert the remaining magnetic prongs into the slits. Open the bottom flap again, and insert the prongs through the metal disk. Hammer down one prong, then hammer the next one over the other bent prong. Finally, glue the suede edge over the python.

12 Refold the bottom section, and begin making marks for the holes. Mark seven holes spaced 1" (3cm) away from the sides and ½" (1cm) apart from each other; repeat for the other side.

Now it is time to start inserting the eyelets into the premade holes. (When inserting the eyelets, please refer to the instructions on the plier tool and the directions on the back side of the fashion eyelets.) Begin placing the first eyelet into the top hole. Place the plier tool inside of the eyelet and press down firmly until you feel a slight crunch. Repeat this step until all holes are filled with eyelets.

13 Cut the ends of the leather strips at a 45-degree angle. (This will allow you to insert the strip easier into the holes.) Insert one of the leather strips through the bottom hole. If the strip is too wide, you can trim it down if you need to.

Make sure that you are lacing out and then around. Think of wrapping the leather strip around covering up the edges of the clutch. Pull the lace all the way through until you have about ½" (1cm) of strip left at the end. Glue that end to the clutch. Then lace through, inside to back. Cut off any excess, and glue the remaining strip end to the clutch. Repeat on the other side.

Glam-Rock Drawstring Purse

When I started to create this bag, I wanted something flashy and cool. I wanted it to be glamorous and have a girly punk flavor. These two looks merged to create a fused rock-stylistic purse. I painted the bag in a bright gold color and accented it with chain and eyelets for a punk rock chic. This bag may look complicated, but you'll be able to pull it off. Don't get me wrong; it will take some time to put together—but when you are finished, you will have a gorgeous girly-tough bag. This purse is meant to show off your individuality, so incorporate some of your old jewelry as embellishments. (I used vintage crystal brooches and random charms.) Or visit thrift stores, garage sales and even antique malls for those rare, one-of-a-kind salvaged pieces.

MATERIALS LIST

15" × 20" (38cm × 51cm) piece of tan hide

2 ⅓" × 15" (6cm × 38cm) piece of tan hide

Tan leather strips, 2 strips ½" × 15" (1cm × 38cm), 4 strips ¼" × 15" (6mm × 38cm) and 1 strip 2" × 20" (5cm × 51cm)

2 silver rings, 2 ⅛" (5cm)

12" (30cm) silver chain

4 rhinestone chains, 9" (32cm) each

Leather and suede glue

Temporary adhesive spray

Tape

Wood board or other hard surface

Various silver charms and beads

1 dangling shell charm

2 vintage crystal brooches

82 silver eyelets

9 silver jump rings

Gold metallic paint

Ballpoint pen

Craft hammer

Eyelet pliers

Leather hole punch

Paintbrush

Artist palette

Needle-nose jewelry pliers

Rotary cutter

Cutting mat

Straightedge

Clear plastic circles template

*I used Tandy Leather Factory Tan Leather Hide and a C-Thru Ruler with circle templates.

LIKE THE SHIRT?
Project instructions can be found on page 30.

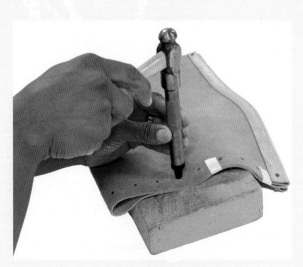

Punch holes in the leather making sure they are evenly spaced.

sweet note

Make sure that you go all the way through the leather when you are punching the holes so you punch out the bottom piece of leather as well.

project instructions

1 Start with the 15" × 20" (38cm × 51cm) and the 2 ⅓" × 15" (6cm × 38cm) pieces of leather. Apply gold metallic paint on the leather with your paintbrush. Cover the area with a nice, even coat. Set aside and let dry. Turn the larger piece of painted leather over to the unpainted side.

2 Make a mark 1" (3cm) from the top. Apply a line of leather and suede glue across the leather. Then fold over until the leather meets the mark and press down for about fifteen seconds.

Repeat this step on the bottom. Set aside and let dry. Make sure to apply two coats of paint to the surface so none of the tan shows through.

3 Place the smaller strip of leather on your cutting mat. Measure out 5½" (14cm) and mark. With your straightedge and rotary tool, cut out laces. Cut the leftover strip in half and set it aside.

4 Turn the big piece of painted leather inside out. Gently fold in half—do not crease. Measure about ½" (1cm) from the sides. Make seven marks downward, 1" (3cm) apart. Repeat on the other side. At the top, measure 1" (3cm) from the side. Make nine marks across, ½" (1cm) apart. Tape the sides together to hold them in place.

5 Place the folded leather on top of a hard surface. Starting about ½" (1cm) from the top with your leather punch and hammer, punch out all of the holes. Keep the holes straight and even. If you don't, the purse will look lopsided.

6 Once you have finished punching out holes, tie a knot at one end of the ½" × 15" (1cm × 38cm) piece of leather and pull through the holes, starting at the bottom hole. Lace upward, pulling the leather like you would pull up shades or blinds. After you have laced the first side, tug at the leather strip and let the leather gather. Make a knot. Tie off the remaining lace, but do not cut off. Repeat the same steps on the other side. The ruched look gives the bag its form and sets the tone. (Ruching is just a fancy way of saying gathered.)

7 Once you have laced the sides, turn the bag outside in. (I love this part because you can see the purse starting to shape.) Make sure that you press the sides of the bag outward as much as you can; this will give the bag its shape. Now that you have pressed out the sides, place a fashion eyelet into the remaining 18 holes along the top edge of the bag. When you load your eyelet pliers, the metal side facing outward, press down firmly until you feel it crunch. Repeat the process until all 18 holes are filled.

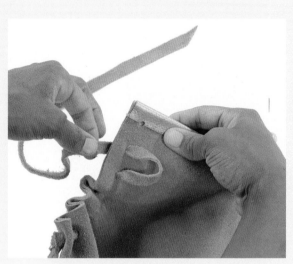

Lace the sides.

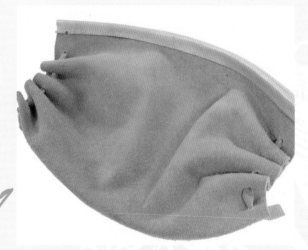

Tug the leather strips so the sides gather, then knot the strips.

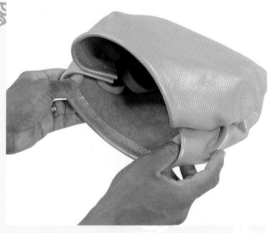

Turn the bag outside in.

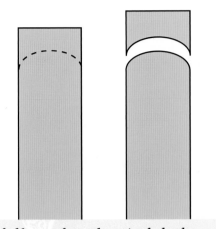

Trace a half-moon shape, then trim the leather to create rounded ends.

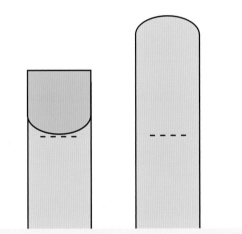

Fold the round end over about 2" (5cm) and mark where it hits. Spray the end past this mark with adhesive.

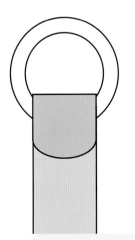

Fold the end over the silver ring and press down.

8 Decide where the back of the bag is, find the eighth eyelet and start lacing through the first with the ¼" × 15" (6mm × 38cm) lace. Using jewelry pliers, pull the lace all the way through until you have more than one inch (3cm) left and make a knot. Resume lacing and pull the leather lace until the bag starts to gather. You will be lacing only the left side. Continue until you get to the front of the bag. (Leave *one* eyelet open at the very front of the bag to attach charms later.) Turn the bag around to the back. Find the eighth eyelet hole, located toward the middle of the bag's back side, and pull through the remaining piece of ¼" × 15" (6mm × 38cm) leather cord. Repeat the same steps with the remaining eyelet holes.

9 Once you've finished lacing, pull the strings gently and allow the bag to gather some more. This will give you an indication on what the bag will look like. For the remaining hole eyelet, lace one end of a leather cord through, then with the help of the jewelry pliers, pull the other end through the same eyelet. Open the inside of the bag and pull the cords until you have a small loop on the front side of the bag. This little loop will be where you can hang all of the chain, bling and charms. Tie the laces together, but be careful not to pull too tight because you will make your loop too small.

10 To make the strap of the purse, you will need the 2" × 20" (5cm × 51cm) piece of leather. Turn over to the unpainted side and use a circle template and pen to trace a half-moon shape. Cut along the mark. This will give the strap its rounded edge. Repeat at the other end. Fold the rounded end over about 2" (5cm), then mark where the tip hits. Be sure that you are folding it inward so that you see the painted end meet the suede side. Spray a light coat of adhesive spray, fold the end over the silver ring to the marked point, and press down lightly; repeat on the other end.

11 Turn the strap over to the painted side and make five marks. Place the strap on a wooden board or hard surface. Starting at one end, measure ½" (1cm) from the side. Make the first mark going across, and then make a second mark 1" (3cm) apart. Make 22 marks 1" (3cm) apart. Once you have finished making marks, use the leather hole punch and craft hammer to punch out each mark.

12 Once the marks are done, insert the silver fashion eyelets into the holes with the pliers tool. Take the two ½" × 15" (1cm × 38cm) laces and cut down the middle so that you have four ¼" (6mm) leather laces. Start by inserting one lace at the end into the first hole of the group of the four holes at the bottom of the strap. Choose which hole you will start with, and insert the lace and tie a knot at the end to secure lace. Now begin lacing upward in a zigzag pattern. Repeat the same process on the other side. You will have an "X" pattern repeating on the strap. Do not tie off the ends of the lace yet.

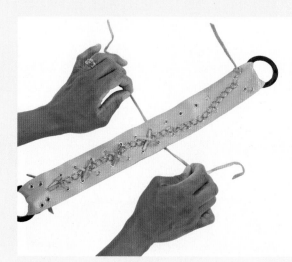

Create an "X" pattern.

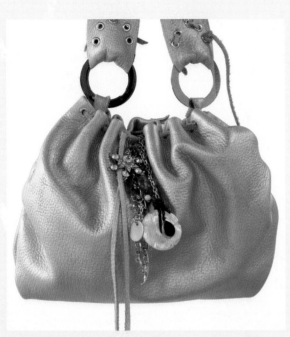

Attach rhinestones, chains, beads and other finds to the loop on the front of the bag.

13 Use the loose leather lace of the inside of the purse to attach the silver rings. Tie double knots to hold the rings to the purse. Insert one end of the strap inside one of the rings. Match up the eyeleted holes together. Thread one of the remaining laces into the bottom group of holes, and then work your way in and out, until you get to the third hole. With the silver chain, insert the exposed lace and thread through the first chain link. Then resume threading the lace through the remaining eyeleted holes. Tie off lace at the end. With the chain, thread under the "X" patterns. Once you get to the other side, repeat the step.

14 Remember the looped piece of leather lace at the front? Attach rhinestone chains, beads and other finds to the loop to give your purse that kick-butt glamour appeal.

Urban Graphic Satchel

As you can see, I like using black and white to accentuate color in my designs. This little handbag has brilliant energy with cool collaborations of textures and supple suedes and leathers. It has a high impact of color and composition. The look of this bag has an ethnic effect and appeal with handmade, earthy touches. The hanging charms finish off the bag—and you can take them off and wear them as a bracelet or on your jeans.

LIKE THE NECKLACE?
Project instructions can be found on page 16.

MATERIALS LIST

Urban Graphic Satchel Templates (page 119)

8½" × 3" (22cm × 8cm) black leather

5½" × 18" (14cm × 46cm) black leather strip

3" × 3" (8cm × 8cm) black leather piece to cover prongs

1 fat quarter yard (46cm × 56cm) yellow and orange sunburst pattern fabric

Cutout of a graphic black-and-white flower

12" (30cm) gold or silver chain

Cardboard or cardstock

Clear tacky spray

Tacky glue

Assorted beads in orange, green and black

Vintage jewelry pieces and findings

Horn

1 large lobster clasp

Melt Art Ultra Thick Embossing Enamel, clear

Black/clear embossing pad

1 skein of embroidery floss in sage green

2 metal rings

Magnetic purse snaps

Black permanent marker

Gold paint pen

Waxed linen thread

Brayer

Eyelet pliers

Heat-set tool for embossing powder

Leather hole punch

Size 22 tapestry needle

Variety of rubber stamps

Scissors

Clothes pins, clip-style

I used Imperial Fusions: EUJ-5905-130 Sunshine by Robert Kaufman, Aleene's Tacky Glue; Gold Sharpie Paint marker; Big & Bossy Black/Clear Embossing Pad; Stamps by Stampington: P2222 Botanica and P2232 Ephemera; Stampin' Up! Butterfly rubber stamp; Heat-it Craft Tool; Aleene's Crystal Clear Tacky Spray; and Anchor tapestry needle.

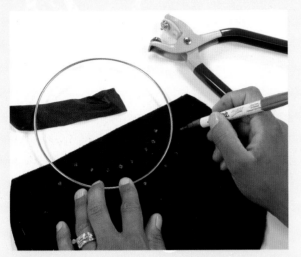

Use the ring handle of the purse to guide the placement of the holes.

Punch out the holes using the eyelet pliers.

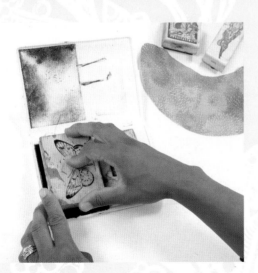

Press firmly to ensure that you get enough embossing ink onto the stamp.

project instructions

1 Photocopy the *Urban Graphic Satchel* template (page 119). Glue to cardboard or cardstock, cut out then trace the round template twice on the leather with the gold permanent marker. Then trace the window template on to the fabric. Set fabric piece aside. Fold round leather pieces down 2" (5cm) from the top. Fold down each piece with the suede side on the outside and the leather (shiny part inside) and glue down folds and roll with the brayer.

2 Pin together the base of the purse with fabric stick pens. Place one ring in the middle of the purse 2" (5cm) from the fold. Make seven marks with the gold paint marker, spaced ½" (1cm) apart, above the ring. Above the marks for the top part of the rings, mark two holes ¼" (6mm) apart. These will be for the magnetic closures. Make eight marks below the ring. These marks are for the rings. Later you will use some leather strips to hold them in place. Make twenty marks ¼" (6mm) around the purse. You will use leather strips to bring the base of the purse together. With the pliers, punch out holes. Set the base of the purse aside.

3 To make the window design, stamp the Butterfly, Botanica and the Ephemera into the black part on the embossing pad. Place stamps on the fabric in any fashion. Keep stamping until you are satisfied with the design.

4 Pour a good amount of the clear Melt Art Ultra Thick Embossing Enamel on top of the stamped fabric. Pour excess back into the bottle and shake off excess. Use the heating tool to heat up the enamel. You'll notice that the enamel will start melting and become shiny. Be very careful because the heat tool gets extremely hot.

5 Apply glue to the center of the fabric artwork, and glue the fabric to the front of the purse, making sure that it is centered. Turn the flower cutout over and glue to the front of the fabric art piece. Draw with the permanent marker around the cutout of the flower. Load your needlepoint needle with the sage green floss. You will begin sewing the edges of the fabric. Start with the needle going in, pull out and then wrap around. Glue the rest of the fabric to the purse.

6 Take one metal ring and wrap once with the leather strip. Place a small amount of glue at the beginning end of the wrapped leather. Attach the clothespin to the part that you wrapped to hold in place. Continue wrapping ring until the ring is covered in leather. Cut the last piece, apply glue and tuck under the wrap. Repeat for the other ring. Tightly wrap the leather to keep secure and glue down each time you get to the end of the leather laces.

Pour out an even amount of Embossing Enamel.

Wrap the leather around the metal ring. Tightly wrap the leather to keep secure and glue down each time you get to the end of the leather laces.

sweet note
Did you pour too much embossing enamel? Simply pour the excess back into the jar.

Assemble the beads and charms on a chain, and then hang them from the front of the purse.

7 Begin lacing up the sides of the purse with a strip of leather. Once the sides are laced, tie off and cut lace. When you get to the end of the lace, glue the end and tuck it under the wrap. Continue lacing again with new lace. Repeat until the purse is held together.

8 Add the rings to the purse in between the upper and lower holes. Insert lace over the rings, and tie together on the inside of the purse. Repeat until the rings are attached to the purse.

9 Insert the magnetic closures prongs into the holes, and insert the prongs through the metal disks. Hammer down one prong, or use jewelry pliers to bend the prongs on top of each other. Glue the leather circle pieces, and cover the exposed prongs on the outside and inside of the fabric.

10 Assemble the charms and beads on the chain. Hang them from the front of the purse over the ring. I used old earrings and took them apart. I love adding beads and charms to a hanging chain. It gives handbags a punch of interest.

Quirky & Charming Pillow Accents

In this chapter you will find cute and surprising projects to suit your taste. You will find kicks of color and whimsy with eclectic, edgy and sophisticated details. Any room will be transformed from boring to amazing when you develop your ability to create hand-stitched, one-of-a-kind accented works of heart!

Chic Stripes Pillow

This pillow screams fun, whimsy and sophistication. I like the way the black design plays off of the colors and stripes. It's perfect for the bed, a couch, or even on the wall framed in a shadow box. Make several to fill up your living space and bring a sophista-funk vibe to your life.

MATERIALS LIST

⅜ yard (.3m) multicolored striped fabric

1 bag of fiber stuffing

2 skeins white embroidery floss

Large black iron-on transfer of choice

White bead paint

Size 18 needle

Sewing machine

*I used Tulip Fashion Bead Paint; Express Yourself Flocked Iron-On Transfer; and Poly-fil stuffing.

sweet note

Pay careful attention when working with striped fabric. Try to match them up and keep them as straight as possible.

Outline the iron-on design with white bead paint.

Sew the pillow together.

project instructions

1 Cut two 16" × 11" (41cm × 28cm) rectangles from the striped fabric. Locate the center of one fabric rectangle, and iron on the transfer, following manufacturer's instructions.

2 Experiment with the bead paint on scrap fabric first to see what size you like. Don't squeeze too hard, or you will get a big ugly blob, not a cute and dainty dot. When you're satisfied with your practice tries, make small dots outlining the iron-on design. At the top and bottom of the iron-on, make one large-size dot and add smaller dots around it. Let dry overnight.

3 Lay the two fabric rectangles on top of each other, right sides together. Pin the rectangles 1" (3cm) from the fabric edge. Leave a 4" (10cm) length unpinned—this will be the hole for turning. Set the tension on your sewing machine to a straight stitch. Sew along the pinned edge.

4 After you have sewn the fabric together, turn the pillow right-side out through the 4" (10cm) hole. Stuff the pillow until it is plump.

5 Hand stitch the opening closed. Thread the needle with embroidery floss, and pull the floss all the way through until you close the opening, then knot the floss at one end of the pillow and begin stitching the pillow together. Continue stitching all the way around the pillow in an over-under manner. After you get to the end of the floss on your needle, sew under the stitches you made to hide the frayed ends. Then, cut as close to the floss as possible.

Flower Blossom Triptych Pillows

These pillows remind me of spices and something warm and yummy. The colors and shapes with the hand-sewn detail give the pillows a bright, modern delight. It's got appealing punchy hues with simple, pretty details. It is so beyond adorable and catches your eye with its collaborations of color and form. The cool, relaxed design gives it crisp, clean symmetry. I adore the gold accents. The mop rings give it a modern and minimalist feel. These pillows are great for the final touches for any room.

MATERIALS LIST

10" × 10" (25cm × 25cm) piece of blue and green feather print fabric

10" × 10" (25cm × 25cm) piece of red and gold feather print fabric

10" × 10" (25cm × 25cm) piece of pink, brown and gold and print fabric

Fabric glue

1 bag of fiber stuffing

3 skeins of embroidery floss, one each in light turquoise, sunrise and iris

White or black thread

18 M.O.P. circles

Size 22 tapestry needle

Sewing needle

Fabric scissors

Sewing machine

*I used EUJM-5905-78 Peacock, EUJM-5905-3 Red and EUJM-5905-20 Amethyst by Imperial Fusions from Robert Kaufman; and Poly-fil stuffing.

sweet note

Use whatever fabrics you like for this project. You can even try using old dresses or shirts!

Stuff the pillows with enough batting to give them their square shape.

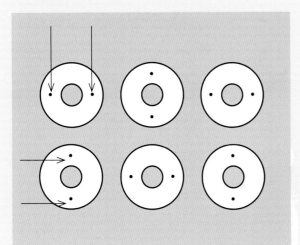

Alternate rings; place some holes sideways and others up-and-down, but keep a clean line pattern.

Sew the holes in the mop circles with embroidery floss.

project instructions

1 Fold the cut pieces of fabric inside out. Place the first piece of fabric under the presser foot and start sewing ½" (1cm) from the edge. Once you get to the last side, leave a 4½" (11cm) gap. Repeat with the other fabrics.

2 Flip the pillows inside out and begin stuffing. Make sure that you push out the corners and fill the pillow as much as you can to give it a square shape. Again, repeat with the other pieces. Load the sewing needle with black or white thread and sew up the open hole on the pillows.

3 Now that the pillows are stuffed, you can place the rings. Decide where the middle is on the pillow. Turn over the mop ring and glue the back. You will notice two holes at each end. Before you glue these down, alternate the holes so that you will create a clean line design with the floss. Place the first mop ring, then repeat until you have a square pattern. The mop rings should be spaced about ¼" (6mm) apart. There should be four disks on the top, middle and bottom. Set aside and let the glue dry.

4 For the next pillow, turn over mop ring and place glue on the back. This time you will only be using three mop rings. Alternate rings by placing the ring holes sideways, up and down, and then sideways to keep the clean line pattern. Glue in a row in the middle of the pillow 1" (6mm) apart. Repeat this step with the last pillow.

5 For the peacock-hued pillow, thread your needle with the light turquoise floss, and sew through the first hole on the mop disk. Once the holes have been filled with floss, you'll have one gorgeous pillow. Repeat this steps with the red pillow using the sunrise floss. For the amethyst pillow, use iris floss. Cut off all of the loose floss to give each pillow a polished look.

Strange Botany Pillow

For this pillow, I wanted an unusual motif that would make a great conversation piece. This pillow has great symmetry, with a mesh of surprising objects, details and organic forms. The black-and-white pattern interacts with the colorful flowers in a playful and dramatic way. This design has energetic graphic locked quality and merges two different looks with painterly effects and perfect balance. I love using bright color and texture to convey an evocative message. May this whimsical pillow brighten your day and make you smile!

LIKE THE CUFF?
Check out page 42 for instructions.

MATERIALS LIST

Strange Botany Pillow template (page 121)

2 pieces 22½" × 12½" (57cm × 32cm) black and white geometric print fabric

2 pieces white fabric, 7" × 9" (57cm × 32cm)

10" × 16" (25cm × 41cm) piece of cardboard

Fiberfill

Clear tape

⅛ teaspoon (.6ml) each of Lumin-Arte Primary Elements in Passion, Jasmine, Key Lime and Sunburst

½ teaspoons (2.5ml) Simple Solutions No. 1 Soft Acrylic Medium for each color, 2 teaspoons (10ml) total

Black permanent marker

Iron-on transfer pen

White thread

Size 14 needle

Paintbrushes, No. 4 round stain, No. 4 flat stain and ¾" (2cm) flat glaze

Artist palette

Sewing machine

Stick pins

I used Color Beat AJS-5741-1 Black by Jennifer Sampou from Robert Kaufman Fabrics.

Paint the flower petals using alternating colors.

Project Instructions

1 Photocopy the *Strange Botany* template on page 121, place one 9" × 7" (18cm × 23cm) piece of fabric over the photocopy. Trace the flower with a black marker. Turn over the photocopy (if you can't see the lines, trace the flower with a dark marker), and trace the flower again with a black marker. Place flower panels on a piece of cardboard. Tape down the top and bottom edges.

2 Scoop out ⅛ teaspoon (.6ml) of Primary Elements Passion, Jasmine, Key Lime and Sunburst in separate sections of your palette. Starting with Passion, mix ½ teaspoon (2.5ml) of Simple Solutions No. 1 Soft Acrylic Medium into the powder and stir until smooth. With the round stain brush, apply color to one petal at a time alternating petals, set aside and let dry. Add ½ teaspoon (2.5ml) of Simple Solutions No. 1 to the Passion powder, and mix until smooth. Clean brush thoroughly with water. With the same brush, apply passion paint to the blank petals, set aside and let dry.

3 Mix ½ teaspoon (2.5ml) of Simple Solutions No. 1 into the Key Lime. Apply paint with the No. 4 flat stain brush to the stem and leaves. Remove tape from panels. Mix ½ teaspoon (2.5ml) Solution No. 1 with Sunburst. Load a ¾" (2cm) flat glaze brush with the mixture, then paint the panels. Try not to paint on top of the flowers. If you can, leave a little white space around design. Set aside and let dry for thirty minutes. After the panels are dry, use a black marker to heavily outline all the lines. This will make the designs and colors pop. With the marker, begin making random circles inside of the flowers and on the outside of the leaves. Then make the stripes and lines inside of the vines and leaves. Paint the inside of the circles with white fabric paint.

sweet note

After each use, clean brushes thoroughly. Even a little bit of leftover paint can muddy up pure color.

4 Once the panels are dry, place them on top of the 22½" ×12" (51cm × 32cm) piece of fabric. Center the panels. Measure about 3" (8cm) away from the edge of the fabric, and place your panels. Make sure there's a 1" (3cm) gap between panels. Make crop marks on the fabric. Turn panels over and spray with temporary adhesive and place panels on crop marks, smoothing out any bubbles.

5 To create a decorative, stitched border along the panels, set your sewing machine to the zigzag setting. Place the fabric under the machine, with the panels facing upward. Sew downward along the edges of the panels, going down the corners in a clockwise direction. Repeat this step on the last panel.

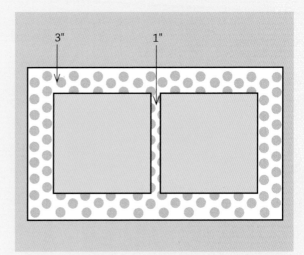

Center the panels so they are 3 inches (8cm) from the top and bottom, and 1 inch (3cm) from each other.

6 Place the fabric pieces on top of each other, making sure the right side of the fabric is facing in. Pin the fabric together around each side. Set your sewing machine to a straight stitch.

7 Place the pillow under the sewing machine presser foot, leaving ½" (1cm) between the pins and the presser foot. That way you won't run over them and injure yourself or your machine. Sew downward, removing pins as you go. Sew all the way around until you reach the bottom corner; leave 4 inches (10cm) open. Fold down one part of the fabric and secure it with pins. Sew the fabric down to itself, and repeat on the other side. Flip the fabric right-side out, then stuff the pillow. Once you have achieved the desired look, finish sewing the fabric together.

sweet note
If you aren't comfortable forcing the fabric closed while machine stitching, try to hand-stitch the opening closed.

Once you have stuffed the pillow to the desired look, finish sewing the fabric together.

Soul-full of Art

Art. I love the word because it says a lot. Art is an expression of self and of life. Like life, it embraces contrasts and harmonies: cheerful colors with stark subjects, for example, or limited color for ornate, intricate designs. As artists, we can show the world all the color and light and energy inside us. And that is why art is beautiful.

Modern Art Gallery Canisters

I saw these canisters on a TV show last year, and I thought to myself, "What a cool product—I wonder what I could do with them?" I wanted to utilize the functionality of the canisters, and enhance the contemporary, streamlined look. So I came up with a cool design and finished off the look with a high-impact teal and subtle hints of brown, blue, gray and white beads to tie it all together.

MATERIALS LIST

2 10" × 20" (25cm × 51cm) blank canvases

Picture frame hanging set

2 sets of spice canisters

Beads of various tints and hues in blues, browns, whites and grays

3 skeins of embroidery floss, one each in brown, teal and light turquoise

2 ounces (57g) Terra Bella Finishes Opulence in Teal

Glue

Black pen

Pencil

Size 22 tapestry needle

Paintbrush

Ruler

I used The Container Store Spice Canisters; Anchor Floss in Chocolate, Teal and Light Turquoise; and an Anchor tapestry needle.

After gluing down the metal strips, sew around the ridges with embroidery floss.

Fill the canisters with beads and other embellishments.

project instructions

1 Paint the canvases with Opulence Teal. Make sure to paint the sides of the canvas as well.

2 Once the canvases are dry, turn over and draw a line 4" (10cm) from the top. On the vertical part of the frame, find the middle, and make mark. Insert the hook into the mark. Insert the wire into the hook and loop it around hook until it's secure. Repeat this on the other side. Do the same with the remaining canvases.

3 Place the metal strip in the middle of the canvases making sure that they line up. Using a pencil, lightly outline the metal strips onto the canvas. Turn over the metal strip, apply glue, flip over and carefully place back into the outlined area. Press the strip into the canvas, then let dry.

4 Once the glue is dry, thread your needle with the first color of embroidery floss. Sew around the ridges of the metal strip. Sew 4–5 times around and secure the floss on the backside by sewing back through the floss and tying it off. Alternate colors.

5 Fill canisters with beads and other finds. Place canisters on sections of the metal strip in alternating levels.

sweet note

The more you make, the better. Try all sorts of combinations. Fill each container with different colors, or change the color of the canvas.

Lady in the Window

For me, this piece evokes the emotion of love, and celebrates womanhood and creativity. It has dimension, beautiful color, bold graphic stamps and great composition. I like how there is more to the artwork every time you look at it. The wooden circles add interest and draw you right in. When you create this piece, use what moves you. Enjoy your time making this piece and let it spark your imagination!

MATERIALS LIST

8" × 6" (20cm × 15cm) shadow box

3 round wooden nickel disks, 1 ⅝"

1 round wooden disk, ⁵⁄₁₆"

3 small wooden squares (the size of a game piece)

Embossing enamel powder in clear and platinum

Embossing pad in clear/black

Alcohol inks in plum, blue, light green and burgundy

Adirondack Alcohol Ink Metallic Mixatives in silver and gold

3 rubber stamps

Glue

Heat-setting tool for embossing powders

I used Ultra Thick Embossing Enamel in clear and platinum; Adirondack Alcohol Inks in Wild Plum, Denim, Lettuce and Cranberry; Adirondack Alcohol Ink Metallic Mixatives in silver and gold; Stampington & Company in P2222 Botanica and P2232 Ephemera; Stampin' Up! Butterfly rubber stamp; Big & Bossy™ Black/ Clear Embossing Pad; and Heat it Craft Tool.

Apply the stamped designs in different layers.

Blow hot air over the enamel until it starts to melt.

project instructions

1 Take out the paper from the shadow box and turn over. This paper will be the base for your artwork.

2 Stamp the Botanica design into the black ink, then transfer the design anywhere on the paper three to four times. Repeat with the other stamps.

3 Once the paper is covered with stamps, spread an even coat of the clear embossing enamel over the paper. Pour the excess back into the embossing container. Shake off the excess enamel.

4 Plug in the Heat it Craft Tool, and heat up the enamel by moving the Heat it Craft Tool over artwork in circular motions. Try not to hold the Heat it tool too close to the paper for too long, because it may either burn your work or crinkle the paper. The enamel should start to melt. This will be your indication that the enamel has embossed your work. Let it cool off, and set it aside.

5 Add color to the paper to fill up some white space. Start with Wild Plum and then alternate colors to create the look and color combinations that you want. Let dry and set aside. Add the silver and gold mixative to your design. Let the colors run into each other, creating a beautiful balance of color and unique design. Once it has dried, turn it over and apply glue and place the glue side down on top of the wooden backing of the shadow box.

6 Apply silver and gold mixative to small parts on the larger wooden disks. Leave space available for the other colors. Stamp two of the disks, then emboss using platinum embossing enamel. Use the Heat it Craft Tool to heat up the enamel. When you use the Heat it Craft Tool, be patient and be careful. The wood will absorb the heat, thus taking its sweet time to cure.

Place the mixative in random places on the artwork.

Glue the wooden disks to the art.

7 Stamp the smaller wooden circle with the Ephemera stamp with the black side on the embossing pad, and add a little cranberry to the lips.

8 Turn artful disks over and apply a drop of glue. Set the small wooden pieces on top of glue, set aside and let dry.

9 After glue has dried, apply glue to the other side of the wooden square pieces and glue down on top of artwork. Make sure that the pieces are aligned and centered. Secure backing of the shadow box and close latches.

Organic Dawn Painting

When I came up with this design, I let it flow. I just kept drawing until I was happy with the composition. The meaning behind this painting is simple really. The colored flowers and branches represent life and beauty. The fire on this side represents purity. Fire purifies and cleanses. The purple side represents loneliness. The flock design symbolizes the moon. The moon still gives off light, but it has no warmth to it. I know, kinda weird, but this is what it means to me and I just love it. When you make this painting, you can do what you want with it. Make it your own individual personal piece. Feel free to change or add anything you like to convey your emotions.

MATERIALS LIST

18" × 10" (46cm × 25cm) canvas

LuminArte Primary Elements Coloring System, 2 teaspoons (10ml) Passion, 2 teaspoons (10ml) Hot Cinnamon, 1 teaspoon (5ml) Mayan Gold

4 tablespoons (60ml) Primary Elements Simple Solutions Acrylic Medium

Black plastic rhinestones

1 white flocked iron-on transfer

Tracing paper

Sulky black iron-on transfer pen

Clear tape

Iron

Artist palette

¾" (2cm) flat glaze paintbrush

3 white paint markers

Fine point permanent markers in blue, green, pink, yellow, orange, purple and black

Glue

Gold permanent marker

I used Tulip Express Yourself! Natural Flocked Iron-On Transfer; Loew-Cornell Artist palette; Loew-Cornell ¾ (2cm) flat glaze White Nylon paintbrush; and Sharpie Paint Markers in White and Gold; and Sharpie Fine Point permanent markers.

sweet note
When using the Primary Elements Simple Solutions, remember the more you use, the more it will dilute your color so be careful. But use enough to make the colors pop.

Paint the canvas with two contrasting colors.

Make the painting your own by adding details with permanent markers and other embellishments.

project instructions

1 If you're tracing a design from somewhere, such as one from the back of the book, use tracing paper and a black marker to trace the design, then turn over and retrace with the iron-on transfer pen. Set aside.

2 Mix the Primary Elements Simple Solutions in your artist palette with Passion mixture color. Paint half of the canvas with the Passion; let dry. Now mix the Primary Elements Simple Solutions in your artist palette and paint the other side with Cinnamon and Mayan Gold. Paint a gradient by blending the Mayan Gold with the Cinnamon. To achieve this look, paint the Mayan Gold color first, then blend in the Cinnamon to give it its rich color. Or you can paint the Cinnamon first, then the Mayan Gold for a beautiful, rich gold tone.

3 Now is the time to place your design. If you're drawing the design, draw a series of branches on the canvas, with leaves and flowers. Make hatch marks on branches and some leaves.

If you traced the design and used the iron-on pen, place the traced design on top of the canvas and iron on the design. Make sure that the iron is on medium high. Iron in a circular motion, being careful not to burn the canvas. At times, hold still in one place for about four seconds. Lift to see if design has transferred.

4 Outline the design with the white paint marker. Color the flowers and other designs in any colors and combination that you like. Add detail with the permanent marker and gold marker.

5 Place the flock design on the purple side of the canvas in the middle. Follow the directions for the flock iron-on.

6 Place glue in any of the circles of the design, and add black rhinestones.

Templates Appendix

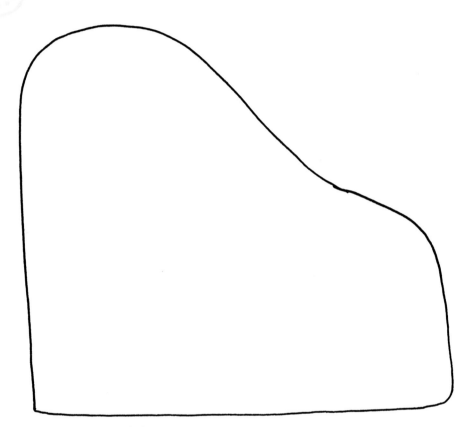

Haze of Green Cell Phone Bag

page 76

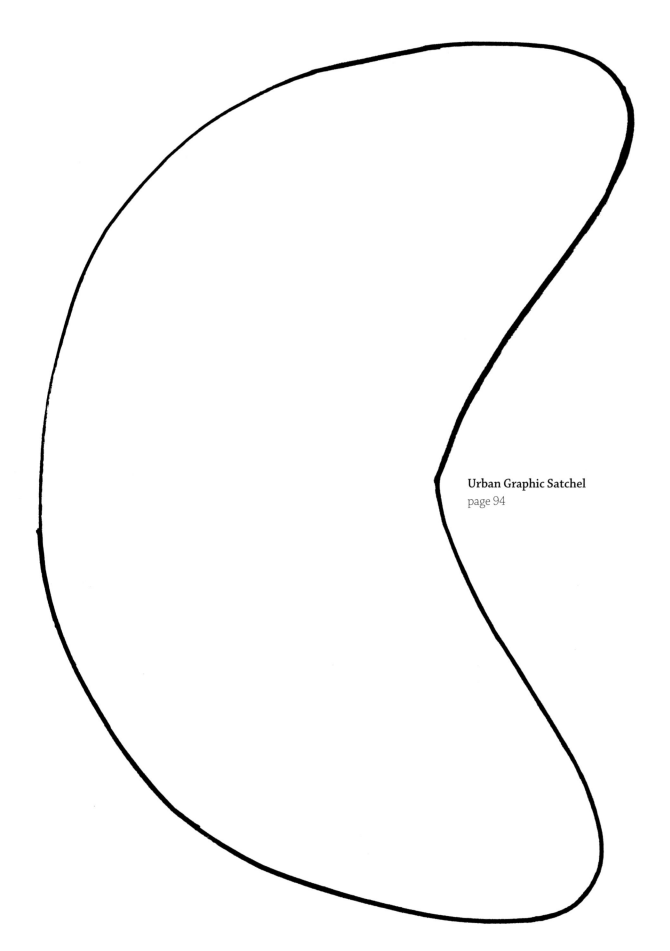

Urban Graphic Satchel
page 94

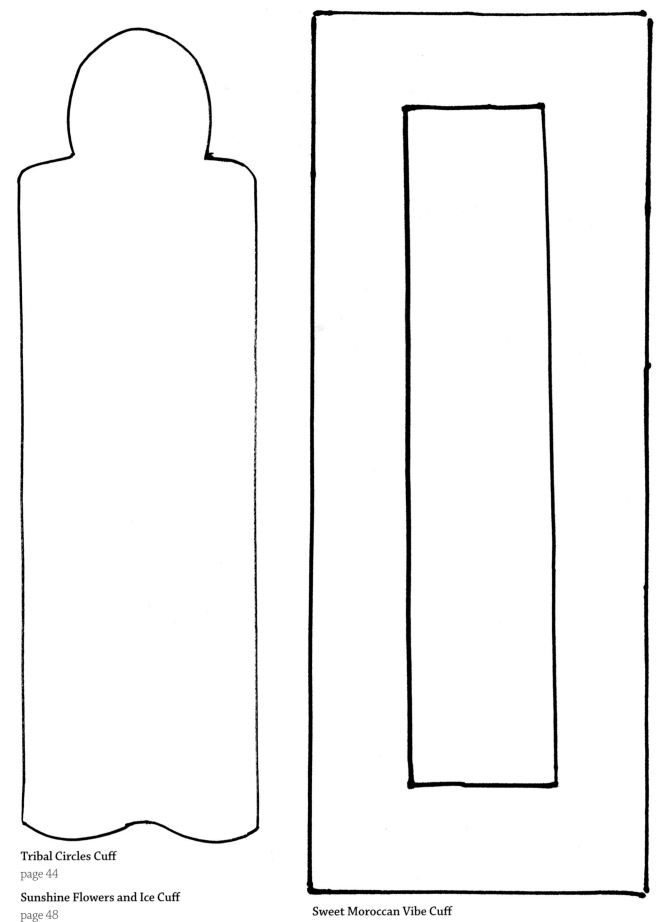

Tribal Circles Cuff
page 44

Sunshine Flowers and Ice Cuff
page 48

Sweet Moroccan Vibe Cuff
page 56

Strange Botany Pillow
page 104

Gilded Flower Tattoo Jeans
page 38

Rocker Hearts and Sweet Butterflies Jeans
page 36

Rocker Hearts and Sweet Butterflies Jeans
page 36

Skater Chic Hoodie
page 30

Skater Chic Hoodie
page 30

Skater Chic Hoodie
page 30

Skater Chic Hoodie
page 30

Skater Chic Hoodie
page 30

Skater Chic Hoodie
page 30

Fabulous Suppliers

Coats & Clark
Floss, needles and threads
P.O. Box 12229
Greenville, SC 29612
(800) 648-1479
www.coatsandclark.com

The Container Store
Magnetic canisters and storage
500 Freeport Parkway
Coppell, TX 75019
(888) 266-8246
www.containerstore.com

Duncan Enterprise
Tulip Paint, adhesives and crystals
5673 E. Shields Avenue
Fresno, CA 93727
(800) 438-6226
www.duncancrafts.com

Loew-Cornell
Paintbrushes
400 Sylvan Avenue
Englewood Cliffs, NJ 07632
(201) 836-7070
www.loew-cornell.com

LuminArte, Inc.
Primary Element paints
3322 W. Sussex Way
Fresno, CA 93722
(559) 229-1544
www.luminarteinc.com

Michael Miller Fabrics LLC.
Fabric
118 West 22nd Street, 5th Floor
New York, NY 10011
(212) 704-0774
www.michaelmillerfabrics.com

Plaid Enterprises, Inc
Hip Stitch Embroidery and Jeaneology iron-on transfers
3225 Westech Drive
Norcross, GA 30092
(800) 842-4197
www.plaidonline.com

Poly-fil
Fiberfill stuffing
Fairfield Processing
P.O. Box 1130
Danbury, CT 06813
(800) 980-8000
www.poly-fil.com

Prym Consumer USA
Sewing notions and embellishments
P.O. Box 5028
Spartanburg, SC 29304
(800) 845-4948
www.dritz.com

Ranger Industries Inc.
Perfect Pearls, embossing, inks and tools
15 Park Road
Tinton Falls, NJ 07724
(732) 389-3535
www.rangerink.com

Robert Kaufman Company, Inc.
Fabrics
P.O. Box 59266, Greenmead Station
Los Angeles, CA 90059-0266
(800) 877-2066
www.robertkaufman.com

Rupert, Gibbon and Spider, Inc.
Fabric dyes, fabric markers and paints
Jacquard Products
P.O. Box 425
Healdsburg, CA 95448
(800) 442-0455
www.jacquardproducts.com

Sanford Brands
Sharpie and Prismacolor art markers and colored pencils
2707 Butterfield Road
Oak Brook, IL 60523
(800) 323-0749
www.sanford.com

Stampington and Company
Art stamps and magazines
22992 Mill Creek, Suite B
Laguna Hills, CA 92653
(949) 380-7318
www.stampington.com

Sulky of America, Inc.
Iron transfer markers and stabilizers
980 Cobb Place Blvd., Suite 130
Kennesaw, GA 30144
(800) 874-4115
www.sulky.com

Tandy Leather Factory
Leather and leather crafting tools
P.O. Box 50429
Ft. Worth, TX 76105-0429
(800) 433-3201
www.tandyleatherfactory.com

Terra Bella Finishes
Faux finishes and paints
P.O. Box 940718
Simi Valley, CA 93094
(800) 771-0602
www.terrabellafinishes.com

Wrights Conso
Trim and tassels
85 South Street
West Warren, MA 01092
(800) 628-9362
www.wrights.com

About the Author

After studying drawing, painting and graphic design at the University of North Texas, I decided that it was time to venture out and start my own small design business. I began selling my works of art to various people through church functions and charity events. One day I envisioned creating a cool, fashionable purse that I had never seen created or manufactured and an idea blossomed. I used a perfume box, glued some of my watercolor paintings to the box and voila! I was on to something! People started noticing my original, one-of-a-kind creations and wanted to know where I bought them. I finally decided to approach boutiques to carry my works of art. To my surprise many of the stores that I approached wanted to carry my creations.

A year passed and I decided to pursue another venture—jewelry making. Before I knew it, it had evolved into a full-time hobby/job. Everywhere I went, people wanted to buy my jewelry and purses right off of me. At that point I realized that others were as excited about wearing my artistic creations as I was making them. Over time, my love and talent for fashion accessories began to mature. I taught myself how to sew and added more complex designs to my bags. One day, I decided to contact Duncan Enterprises and let them know what I was doing with their products. I e-mailed them my Web site and—*boom!*—we started a wonderful relationship. They loved my work so much that they asked me to be one of their "Celebrity Designers" at the 2007 Winter CHA (Craft and Hobby Association). I had a blast and met some wonderful people.

My faith in Christ has sustained and grounded me. I love the Lord so much that I find his Word radiating through my works of art. Through my passion, the Lord has given me the gift of communication, creativity, a strong sense of self and a love for people, especially my husband, son Bayley, and daughters, Bella and Jolie. My husband Shane has encouraged me to follow my dreams and reach for the sky.

My works of art have been displayed and sold in more than 30 boutiques and galleries in North Dallas, Chelsea, New York, and San Antonio. It was so cool to finally get some exposure for my work in print and on TV. Here are some shows, magazines and newspapers that have featured my art: *Positively Texas*, KTVT-TV; UPN's national television show *The Daily Buzz*; HGTV's *Crafters Coast to Coast* and *That's Clever*; The Dallas Morning News *Style Makers* and Dallas Morning News *Quick*. My most recent work has been featured in *Adorn Magazine* and *Altered Couture*.

Contact me at candace@candypurse.com and view more cool stuff at www.candypurse.com.

My style has the right mix of offbeat and edgy sophistication that meets up with a punk-rocker chic sting and with a no-holds barred flair. I enjoy weaving in dashes of vibrant colors and spiky elements, such as hand-painted details, rhinestones, Italian leathers, antique and vintage pieces all rolled up in a couture ball of personality. All of this can be seen on handbags, jeans and all types of fashion and home accessories.

Quick and Easy Stitching

Low-Sew Boutique
25 Quick & Clever Projects
Using Ready-Mades
by Cheryl Weiderspahn
Transform common placemats, towels, potholders and rugs into 25+ innovative fashion accessories, such as a backpack, eyeglass case, and purse by following the detailed instructions and illustrations in this unique guide.

Paperback • 8 ¼ × 10 ⅞
128 p • 175 color photos
Item# Z0378
ISBN-10: 0-89689-434-7
ISBN-13: 978-0-89689-434-1

Sip 'n Sew
20+ Home-Sewn Gifts and Refreshing Drinks
by Diane Dhein
Stitch delightful gifts for family and friends, while serving up delicious drinks, sure to tempt the taste buds! Features 24 projects for the home along with 20 delightful drink recipes, all quick and easy to make.

Paperback • 8 × 8
160 p • 75 color illus.
Item# Z0981
ISBN-10: 0-89689-552-1
ISBN-13: 978-0-89689-552-2

No Sew, Low Sew Decorative Storage
50 Stylish Projects to Stash Your Stuff
by Carol Zentgraf & Elizabeth Dubicki
This collection of 50 inexpensive and easy-to-make storage solutions for the home can be completed with a hot glue gun, basic hand stitches, and other fast and easy techniques. Includes step-by-step instructions and 200 photos.

Paperback • 8¼ × 10 ⅞
144 p • 100+ color photos, 50 illus.
Item# DECST
ISBN-10: 0-87349-889-5
ISBN-13: 978-0-87349-889-0

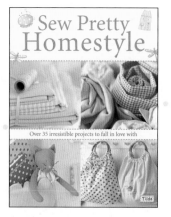

Sew Pretty Homestyle
by Tone Finnanger
A subtle color palette and lovable designs combine to create a fresh and fun collection of over 35 projects.

Paperback • 8½ × 11
144 p • 140 color photos • 100 color illus.
Item# Z0936
ISBN-10: 0-7153-2749-6
ISBN-13: 978-0-7153-2749-4

Sew Easy as Pie
by Chris Malone
This tasty collection of 15 "easy-as-pie" projects for the kitchen is complemented with 8 scrumptious pie recipes that can be baked while projects are stitched. Projects include place mats, napkins, hot pads, curtains, and more.

Paperback • 8 × 8
144 p • 150 color photos
Item# Z0976
ISBN-10: 0-89689-550-5
ISBN-13: 978-0-89689-550-8

Discover imagination, innovation and inspiration at
www.mycraftivity.com.
Connect. Create. Explore.